# CONSTITUTIONAL DOCTRINES OF JUSTICE OLIVER WENDELL HOLMES

# CONSTITUTIONAL DOCTRINES OF JUSTICE OLIVER WENDELL HOLMES

BY

DORSEY RICHARDSON

---

A DISSERTATION

Submitted to the Board of University Studies of the Johns
Hopkins University in Conformity with the Requirements
for the Degree of Doctor of Philosophy
1920

**HYPERION PRESS, INC.**
*Westport, Connecticut*

Published in 1924 by Johns Hopkins Press, Baltimore
Hyperion reprint edition 1981
Library of Congress Catalog Number 79–01618
ISBN 0–88355–921–8
Printed in the United States of America

Library of Congress Cataloging in Publication Data
Richardson, Dorsey, 1896–
  Constitutional doctrines of Justice Oliver Wendell
Holmes.
  Reprint of the 1924 ed. published by Johns Hopkins
Press, Baltimore, which was issued as ser. 42, no. 3 of
Johns Hopkins University studies in historical and
political science.
  Thesis—Johns Hopkins University, 1920.
  Includes bibliographical references.
  1. Holmes, Oliver Wendell, 1841–1935.  2. United
States—Constitutional law.  I. Title.  II. Series: Johns
Hopkins University. Studies in historical and political
science ; ser. 42, no. 3.
KF8745.H6R5 1981      342.73 ′0092 ′4      79–01618
ISBN 0–88355–921–8

# TABLE OF CASES

# TABLE OF CONTENTS

# PREFACE

Oliver Wendell Holmes, II, was born at Boston on March 8, 1841. Son of the Autocrat of the Breakfast Table, and grandson of Charles Jackson, an associate justice of the Supreme Judicial Court of Massachusetts, he inherited the literary bent and the keen judicial mind which have distinguished his career.

He was educated at E. S. Dixwell's private Latin school, Boston, and graduated from Harvard College in 1861, immediately enlisting in the Union army. He served throughout the Civil war with distinction, rising to the permanent rank of Captain, and brevet Lieutenant-Colonel, in the 20th Massachusetts Infantry. He was wounded three times, at Ball's Bluff, Antietam, and Mayre's Hill. After three years of strenuous battle service, he became aide to Brigadier-General (afterwards Major-General) H. G. Wright, and served in that capacity until discharged.

At the conclusion of his military career, he entered the Harvard Law School, graduating in 1866. The next year he began the practice of law in Boston with his brother, Edward Jackson Holmes, since deceased. From 1870 to 1872 he lectured on Constitutional law and Jurisprudence at Harvard Law School, and edited the American Law Review, writing many important articles and reviews for that publication. In 1873 he became associated with the law firm of Shattuck, Holmes and Monroe, and continued in the practice of law for the next nine years. His reputation at the Suffolk Bar was of the highest.

In 1882, he became a full professor in the Harvard Law School, but left his chair after a few months to become an Associate Justice upon the Supreme Judicial Court of Massachusetts, in which capacity he served until August 2, 1899. He then was appointed Chief Justice. In December, 1902,

President Roosevelt named him as an Associate Justice of
the Supreme Court of the United States, to fill the vacancy
caused by the resignation of Justice Gray.

Comments upon his promotion in the periodicals of the
day were unanimously favorable.  The reputation for great
learning and the highest judicial qualities which he had made
in Massachusetts caused the legal profession generally to
express itself as pleased with his elevation to the Supreme
Court.

The one sustained work of which he is the author is " The
Common Law," published in 1881.  Contemporary reviews
greeted it as the most important addition to the literature of
legal commentary since Maine's " Ancient Law," and for
nearly thirty years it has been regarded as a classic.  The
material contained in the volume was partially set forth in
articles in the American Law Review during 1871-1873, and
later rewritten and delivered as a course of lectures at the
Lowell Institute in Boston during 1880.

Justice Holmes edited the 12th edition of Kent's Commentaries, published in 1873, adding many voluminous and
valuable notes.

During his career on the bench, he has written frequent
articles for legal journals, important among them being several dealing with the law of torts.  He is regarded by some,
notably Professor Wigmore of Northwestern University, as
the originator of the present habit of treating that subject
as a separate branch of the law.  The articles which he has
published from time to time have recently been collected, and
are announced for immediate publication in book form.

His occasional speeches, delivered over a period of thirty-
five years, have been collected and privately printed by Justice Holmes, for circulation among his friends.  To appreciate his many-sided literary and legal genius one needs to
read this volume.

The limited scope of the following study prevents the consideration of many of the most delightful characteristics
which Justice Holmes has exhibited in his literary and judi-

cial works. A companion study of probably greater interest
and value might be made of the "literary" opinions of
Justice Holmes. Some of his writings, hidden away among
the reports of the Supreme Court, are worthy of the Autocrat at his best, and abound in literary skill of the highest
type. One finds the artist and the philosopher, rather than
the conventional judge, in such opinions as Bleistein vs. Don-
aldson Lithographing Company,[1] White-Smith Publishing
Company vs. Apollo Company,[2] and Herbert vs. Shanley
Company.[3]

Some of the respects in which he differs from the ordinary
judge are to be seen by a comparison of his opinion in the
Bleistein case with that of Justice Harlan.

The study here presented deals with only the most important of the constitutional questions upon which Justice Holmes
has expressed his opinion. In many of these cases Justice
Holmes has held views differing from those of the court, and
it has been with reluctance that a consideration of them has
been omitted in this study. His opinions in Admiralty cases
have evidenced a clear and consistent understanding of the
history and development of that branch of the law, and even
in dissent have been of profound influence.[4] One of his dissenting opinions interpreting the Full Faith and Credit
Clause of the Constitution has shown a unique position.[5] In
the field of patent, copyright, and trade-mark he has delivered notable opinions.[6]

It should be said that this study was prepared in 1920,
but, for various reasons, its publication was delayed until the
present time.

D. R.

---

[1] 188 U. S., 239.
[2] 209 U. S., 1, J. Holmes concurring, 18.
[3] 242 U. S., 591.
[4] Especially important is his dissent in So. Pac. S. S. Co. vs. Jensen, 244 U. S., 205, 218.
[5] Haddock vs. Haddock, 201 U. S., 562; J. Holmes diss., 628.
[6] For instance, the Bleistein, Herbert and White-Smith cases, and
the Waterman pen cases, 235 U. S., 88.

# CONSTITUTIONAL DOCTRINES OF JUSTICE OLIVER WENDELL HOLMES

## CHAPTER I

### INTRODUCTION

The explanation of conclusions reached by any legal philosopher is not to be made without reference to his premises. A starting point for his system of law must be found—a general conception of the source and nature of all law. In the light of this, his conclusions are illuminated.

The problem of classifying Justice Holmes as to his philosophical school is a difficult one. His avowed beliefs as to the nature of law fall neither wholly within the analytical, historical or sociological schools, nor wholly without them. They form, rather, a philosophy of the law which, built upon fact, develops on practical rather than logical lines.

The Austinian definition of law—as a command of a political superior to a political inferior—he accepts in so far as it applies to "what lawyers call law." But on philosophical grounds he rejects the definition as too narrow. That only what is accepted and enforced by the courts is law,—Justice Holmes believes to be a practical statement rather than a philosophical one. The point upon which he differs from the Austinian conception seems to be this; Austin held that the courts, in all their acts, were representing the sovereign, and that therefore their dicta no matter upon what founded, became the commands of the sovereign. Thereafter, the rules laid down by the court were law, while other customs and principles were only a motive for decision, and not properly law until affirmatively accepted by the courts.

Justice Holmes does not distinguish between what has been accepted and promulgated by the courts and what still remains in the category of custom. Both, he believes, are only

11

motives for decision. The following quotation sets forth at some length his criticism of the Austinian theory:

> Austin said, following Heineccius (Recitationes, 72), that custom only became law by the tacit consent of the sovereign manifested by its adoption by the courts; and that before its adoption it was only a motive for decision, as a doctrine of political economy, or the political aspirations of the judge, or his gout, or the blandishments of the emperor's wife might have been. But it is clear that in many cases custom and mercantile usage have had as much compulsory power as law could have, in spite of prohibitory statutes; and as to their being only motives for decision until adopted, what more is the decision which adopts them as to any future decision? What more indeed is a statute; and in what other sense law, than that we believe that the motive which we think that it offers to the judges will prevail, and will induce them to decide a certain case in a certain way, and so shape our conduct on that anticipation? A precedent may not be followed; a statute may be emptied of its contents by construction; or may be repealed without a saving clause after we have acted on it; but we expect the reverse, and if our expectations come true, we say that we have been subject to law in the matter in hand. It must be remembered, as is clear from numerous instances of judicial interpretation of statutes in England and of constitutions in this country, that in a civilized state it is not the will of the sovereign that makes lawyers' law, even when that is its source, but what a body of subjects, namely, the judges, by whom it is enforced, *say* is his will. The judges have other motives for decision, outside their own arbitrary will, beside the commands of their sovereign. And whether those other motives are, or are not, equally compulsory, is immaterial if they are sufficiently likely to prevail to afford a ground for prediction. The only question for the lawyer is, how will the judges act? Any motive for their action, be it constitution, statute, custom, or precedent, which can be relied upon as likely in the generality of cases to prevail, is worthy of consideration as one of the sources of law, in a treatise of jurisprudence.[1]

In a word, Justice Holmes does not give a sacrosanct character to precedent, and believes that all the motives which go to influence a court's decision, whether expressed or inarticulate, should be considered sources of the law. However, as a formal definition of law, in his notes to Kent's Commentaries, he recommends that of Austin.[2]

---

[1] American Law Rev., 723, 724 (1872).

[2] That he still believes substantially in the Austinian conception of law is to be noted in a recent case, Southern Pac. SS. Co. vs. Jensen, 244 U. S., 205, J. Holmes dissenting, 218: "The common law is not a brooding omnipresence in the sky, but the articulate voice of some sovereign or quasi sovereign that can be identified."

The doctrine of " natural law " he sweeps aside in a recent
article in the Harvard Law Review.* He cannot believe in
natural rights of man. In all society, he says, duties and
rights arise from the practical necessity of forbearance, if
men are to live together and exist. But he finds no inherent
right which permits one man to live beside another. The
fact that they do so, and bear and forbear, is based upon
utilitarian considerations. His view of the matter is expressed in these words:

> It is true that beliefs and wishes have a transcendental basis in
> the sense that their foundation is arbitrary. You can not help
> entertaining and feeling them, and there is an end of it. As an
> arbitrary fact, people wish to live, and we say with various degrees
> of certainty that they can do so only on certain conditions. To do
> it, they must eat and drink. That necessity is absolute. It is a
> necessity of less degree but practically general that they should live
> in society. If they live in society, so far as we can see, there are
> further conditions. Reason working on experience does tell us, no
> doubt, that if our wish to live continues, we can do it only on those
> terms. But that seems to me the whole of the matter. I see no
> *a priori* duty to live with others and in that way, but simply a
> statement of what I must do if I wish to remain alive.

If Justice Holmes must be placed in one of the established
schools of jurisprudence, the sociological should be selected.
He has ever emphasized experience, the conditions of the
moment, as the great practical source of law. In his writings, he has adduced historical examples of the changes
wrought in the law by social and economic conditions. The
law to him has been a living thing, shaping itself to meet
the needs of society,—never a dead hand laid upon the present. The working out of a logical theory of jurisprudence
has not been his task. His active life has been constructive,
moulding the existing law into a code applicable to present
problems, and attempting to change those parts of the law
which have become atrophied.

That he has been influenced by the history of law, and
especially the history of the common law, cannot be denied.
The importance of reconciling existing law to some given
theory of jurisprudence has not appeared to him as great as

---

* Natural Law, 32 Harv. Law Rev., 40, 41-42.

reconciling it with life.  While his early legal career gave him occasion to speculate upon the nature and sources of law, his later life since coming to the bench has been devoted to developing the law.

Ignoring the natural law, and with it the contract theory of the state, he finds the origin of state life, and of legal duties and rights, in their utility.  "A legal right is nothing but a permission to exercise certain natural powers," [4] he said long ago.  Antecedent to legal rights, he saw legal duties, and argued strongly for a classification of the whole body of the law into duties and rights. [5]

It is impossible to escape the conviction that the development of the common law, by court and by legislature in England, has profoundly influenced Justice Holmes in his judicial career.  The results he has striven to attain in the law are generally believed to be beneficial to society as a whole.  Indeed, if the law is taken to be in the last analysis an embodiment of justice, there is reason to believe that his approach, partly historical and partly sociological, is perhaps better than that of other judges who have got out of tune with the present.  Whether our constitutional system can be reconciled with the all-powerful legislature of Great Britain remains for the Supreme Court of the United States to work out slowly from time to time.  But that a greater flexibility of either our law or our Constitution is coming to be necessary is admitted by all.  Pointing out this necessity has been a great duty of Justice Holmes.  He has been a reformer in the law, and his efforts have been crowned with success and spent in defeat as have those of other reformers of the past and present.  He has maintained a lofty ideal of his duty, an ideal which will explain his tenacity of purpose and something of his conception of the function of a judge: "Law is the business to which my life is devoted, and I should show less than devotion if I did not do what in me lies to improve

---

[4] Common Law, p. 214.
[5] Ibid., pp. 219, 220; 5 Am. Law Rev., 1, and other articles in the same journal.

it, and, when I perceive what seems to me the ideal of its
future, if I hesitated to point it out and to press toward it
with all my heart." [6]

To Justice Holmes the problem of the jurist is the examination of the history and the justification of rules of law,
determining their real value, and putting them into practical
harmony with life.  To make this examination he employs
historical research.  To form his conclusions of the worth
of a given rule he calls upon science, chiefly sociological science.  He believes in an attitude of "enlightened scepticism" towards a rule of law.  He would trace it historically
to its source, find its reason for being, and then deliberately
consider its worth to the present.  In his words: "When you
get the dragon out of his cave on the plain and in the day-
light, you can count his teeth and claws, and see just what
is his strength.  But to get him out is only the first step.
The next is either to kill him, or to tame him and make him
a useful animal." [7]

The first paragraphs of the "Common Law" give
most clearly Justice Holmes' idea of just what law is and
what it must be, and the basis upon which his desired de-
velopments of the law must be justified.  Experience, modified in modern parlance into science, statistics and political
economy, is the great law giver, and law flowing from any
other source will not endure:

The life of the law has not been logic: it has been experience.
The felt necessities of the time, the prevalent moral and political
theories, intuitions of public policy, avowed or unconscious, even the
prejudices which judges share with their fellow-men, have had a
good deal more to do than the syllogism in determining the rules
by which men should be governed.[8]
There is, too, a peculiar logical pleasure in making manifest the
continuity between what we are doing and what has been done
before.  But the present has a right to govern itself so far as it
can; and it ought always to be remembered that historic continuity
with the past is not a duty, it is only a necessity.
I hope that the time is coming when this thought will bear fruit.
An ideal system of law should draw its postulate and its legislative

---

[6] Path of the Law, 10 Harv. Law Rev., 457, 473.
[7] Ibid., 457, 468-469.
[8] Common Law, p. 1.

justification from science. As it is now, we rely upon tradition, or vague sentiment, or the fact that we never thought of any other way of doing things, as our only warrant for rules which we enforce with as much confidence as if they embodied revealed wisdom.*

Seeing the law as a malleable body, ever changing to give substantial justice to its subjects, Justice Holmes, with a frankness that is sometimes brutal, frequently confesses the inadequacy of a law, or the injustice of it. He is not given to any of the common subterfuges of the bench. The reasons which lead him to invalidate a law or to uphold it are usually stated in his opinion, fully and frankly. He does not content himself with worn-out fictions. He has admitted that almost any result can be reached by formal logic. His opinions are filled with brilliant phrases, and with trenchant definitions. He is everywhere honest with himself and with those who must read his words. He does not hide behind convenient precedents and take the easiest course. So, beneath many of his dissenting opinions, one may see the true basis of his decision, namely, that, whatever the law has been in the past, true justice demands a different interpretation than that given by the majority. Thus, whether one can always agree with Justice Holmes' opinions, one cannot but admire the staunch inflexibility with which he impresses his ideals upon the legal literature of the day.

Succeeding chapters will attempt to set out the practical application of Justice Holmes' broad view of the law, especially as regards the salient features of United States constitutional law. In introduction it is necessary simply to show the point of view from which he approaches his consideration of the Constitution.

Just as he believes that private law is not rigid, he holds that the Constitution is susceptible of change in the interpretation given to it by the courts.

Of course, the determination of how far he would allow the court to go in this process of change is fundamental in a study of this kind. It is sufficient here to say that

---

* Learning and Science, Speeches, pp. 67, 68.

Justice Holmes is not an advocate of change for the sake of novelty, or for some passing whim of public opinion. From his writings one can deduce a pretty definite theory of constitutional interpretation, which he has followed consistently. This theory was expressed first in Massachusetts: "To state in our own way the mode of approaching the question, it is not so important to consider what picture the framers of the constitution had in their minds as what benefits they sought to secure, or evils to prevent,—what they were thinking against in their affirmative requirement . . . and what they would have prohibited if they had put the clause in a negative form." [10]

Some examples will illustrate his consistency in this respect. The Commerce Clause is a plenary grant of power to the Federal government. Whatever it may have meant in 1789, the framers of the Constitution by its provisions trusted the regulation of interstate and foreign commerce to the Congresses of the future. There were no qualifications placed upon it. One of the moving reasons for the grant of power, no doubt, was the chaotic condition of commerce caused by individual tariffs at colonial borders, but it would scarcely be argued that a general grant of power, such as the Commerce Clause, was necessary to correct the evils which had arisen in the past. The power to regulate commerce could not be limited on other historical grounds. The term "regulation" was at that time susceptible of many meanings, and regulatory measures of other nations, and of England especially, had changed with the development of commerce and industry. Therefore, almost any interpretation could be placed upon the commerce clause by Congress, and the Supreme Court would have difficulty in finding that interpretation to be *ultra vires*.

This is the view which Justice Holmes has adopted,—and with some exceptions it has been the view of the Supreme Court. "The benefits which they sought to secure" were

---

[10] Re House Bill No. 1291, Mass., 54 L. R. A., 430.

here plainly those which would arise from a centralized control of commerce.

Likewise, "due process of law" throughout its history has been a phrase to conjure with. Definition of it has been avoided, and its implications have changed with the generations. When Justice Holmes came to the bench, it was a firm principle of the constitutional law that due process was a flexible term, capable of enlargement or contraction as the necessity arose. Consequently, he has battled against the establishment of a set meaning for it. As it developed in the past history of our law, he believes it should be allowed to develop in the future.

However, where there has been a well-defined interpretation given to a provision of the Constitution, where that interpretation has been accepted throughout our legal history and that of our legal antecedent, Justice Holmes finds that an arbitrary change is not to be justified under ordinary circumstances. Thus, he refuses to enlarge the meaning which has been given for three hundred years, in England and the United States, to the words of the 8th Amendment, prohibiting "cruel and unusual punishments." By the test which he applied in Massachusetts,—"the benefits they sought to secure, or evils to prevent,"—he discovers that the 8th Amendment prohibited bodily torture, not punishment cruel because of the length of incarceration, or the lack of proportion between the punishment and the crime. He maintained that framers of the 8th Amendment had only the accepted meaning in mind, that only this meaning had ever been given to the words, since the Bill of Rights of 1688, and that no American court had ever taken a different view. Therefore, he believed it to be outside of the province of the Supreme Court to read an entirely new meaning into the Amendment.[11]

These illustrations show sufficiently the ideas which Justice Holmes brings to his interpretation of the Constitution.

---

[11] Weems vs. U. S., 217 U. S., 349, 382.

Knowing his predilection for harmonizing the law of our fathers with present conditions, we can safely assume that he has been on the side of rational change in constitutional interpretation whenever it was not too plainly an overturning of the purposes of the framers of the fundamental law or of a judicial definition that has been long fixed.

His whole philosophy of constitutional interpretation is summed up in the following paragraph: " But the provisions of the Constitution are not mathematical formulas having their essence in their form; they are organic, living institutions transplanted from English soil. Their significance is vital, not formal; it is to be gathered not simply by taking the words and a dictionary, but by considering their origin and the line of their growth." [12]

The two clauses of the Constitution most prolific of litigation in the past twenty years have been the Commerce Clause and the 14th amendment. As we have noted, Justice Holmes does not find a definite meaning for either of these, and therefore in their interpretation his individuality is most illuminatingly shown.

By the Commerce Clause a significant centralization in Congress has been accomplished; a national police power has been set up to control activities long thought to be within the province of the States alone. By the 14th Amendment, the Federal judiciary has been placed in a position to control state legislation to a marked degree.

Justice Holmes has, in general, acquiesced in the former extension of Federal authority, believing the Commerce Clause capable of expansion on account of its general terms. On the other hand, he has looked with disfavor upon the wholesale invalidation of state police regulations under the 14th Amendment, basing his dissent upon a unique conception of the function of the three coördinate branches of the government.

He classes true police regulations, made for the health and

---

[12] Gompers vs. U. S., 233 U. S., 604.

morals of the community, as matters of policy, and holds that the legislative determination of their desirability and worth is conclusive. So, he has upheld state laws which the majority of the Supreme Court has held unconstitutional under the 14th Amendment.

His efforts have been directed at a new definition of the police powers, Federal and State. The exercise of these powers by the appropriate legislatures, has attempted to bring the law into harmony with the needs of everyday life. The power of the courts, in reviewing regulations under the police power, should be restricted, according to Justice Holmes. He has been consistently unwilling to undertake the revision of legislation, when its foundation has been the police power. As he expressed himself early in his judicial career in Massachusetts, he has acted until today: " In my opinion, the legislature has the whole lawmaking power except so far as the words of the Constitution expressly or impliedly withhold it, and I think that in construing the Constitution we should remember that it is a frame of government for men of opposite opinions and for the future, and therefore not hastily import into it our views, or unexpressed limitations derived merely from the practice of the past." [13]

The important lines to be drawn in the construction of the Constitution have appeared to Justice Holmes, then, not to be those between the state and the nation, so much as those between the court and the legislature, between the rigid and the flexible parts of the Constitution itself.

Finally, Justice Holmes has insisted that the courts, in considering constitutional questions, put aside prejudice and personal opinion, and make effective " dominant opinion." He has been remarkable for the fact that he has enforced laws in which he does not believe, and in enforcing them has voiced his disapproval. One noteworthy example of this characteristic will suffice before a consideration of his opinions is undertaken.

---

[13] Opinion of the Justices, 160 Mass., 586, 594.

In the matter of the so-called Peonage Laws of Alabama, Justice Holmes is found strongly supporting the view that they are constitutional. The law upon which his opinion is expressed came before the court in the case of Bailey vs. Alabama,[14] and was held unconstitutional. It provided that the breach of a contract for personal services, where part of the wages had been advanced and had not been repaid at the time of the breach, should be prima facie evidence of fraudulent intent, and that the laborer if found guilty should be fined and imprisoned.

The argument of the court's opinion, rendered by Justice Hughes, is based largely upon the clause making the breach of contract prima facie evidence of fraud, and thus avoiding the necessity of other proof of an intent to defraud. The burden of proof is thus wrongfully shifted. Moreover, the laborer is forced into an involuntary servitude, since his debt is not a simple debt, but money fraudulently obtained, and under duress of this threat he is coerced into carrying out his contract. Thus, since the purpose of the Alabama law was ultimately compulsory service, and a state may not do indirectly that which it may not do directly, the statute is contrary to the 13th Amendment.

Justice Holmes, with Justice Lurton, objects strongly to this reasoning. It is his belief that if this case had come up from New York, and the statute punished mere refusal to perform a labor contract, it would be held valid. The 13th Amendment does not outlaw contracts for labor.

But any legal liability for breach of a contract is a disagreeable consequence which tends to make the contractor do as he said he would. Liability to an action for damages has that tendency as well as a fine. If the mere imposition of such consequences as tend to make a man keep to his promise is the creation of peonage when the contract happens to be for labor, I do not see why the allowance of a civil action is not, as well as an indictment ending in fine. . . . Breach of a legal contract without excuse is wrong conduct, even if the contract is for labor.

Simply by the addition of a criminal liability to the civil,

---

[14] 219 U. S., 219, J. Holmes dissenting, 245.

the statute does not enslave a laborer, and if a fine may be imposed, it follows that imprisonment may be also imposed. Though the fact undoubtedly is that the criminal provisions of the statute operate as a motive to keep the laborer working when he would like to leave, " it does not strike me as an objection to a law that it is effective."

The stipulation that a breach is prima facie evidence of fraud is supportable constitutionally, since it does not raise a conclusive presumption, but leaves the question to the jury to decide. " In my opinion, the statute embodies little if anything more than what I should have told the jury was the law without it." The state has the right to regulate its own rules of evidence, and the statute does not greatly go beyond the common law.

To sum up, I think that obtaining money by fraud may be made a crime as well as murder or theft; that a false representation, expressed or implied, at the time of making a contract of labor, that one intends to perform it, and thereby obtaining an advance, may be declared a case of fraudulently obtaining money as well as any other; that if made a crime it may be punished like any other crime; and that the unjustified departure from the promised service without repayment may be declared a sufficient case to go to the jury for their judgment; all without in any way infringing the 13th Amendment or the statutes of the United States.

This is a shining example of the thoroughly judicial attitute maintained by Justice Holmes upon cases involving social and political matters. Starting from his premise that law at any given time, coming from the legislature, is a reflection of prevailing public opinion and desire, and not to be held void unless so obviously contrary to the Constitution that no reasonable construction can save it,—and carrying out his often exhibited readiness to give validity to social and economic views which he does not share personally,— Justice Holmes here presents a strong argument for the constitutionality of a statute which reasonably may be held valid, and which embodies in law a remedy for a very real economic fact, the unreliability of negro labor. From his whole career, no one can imagine that Justice Holmes is in sympathy with the oppression of the negro; but equally from his career on the bench, no one can be surprised that he has upheld the right of a community to apply to local conditions a law that is obviously appropriate to them, and, in his opinion, valid, if disassociated from the conception of the oppression of the negro race.

In the light of the tests he applies to the Constitution, Justice Holmes is inclined to find the guarantee of adjective rights to be more rigid than those of substantive rights. In general, he has demanded a literal interpretation of the procedural guarantees of the Amendments based upon inquiry as to what they were intended to prevent at the time of their creation. In subsequent chapters it will be seen that his position in this regard has not been without modification in favor of the practical. He has upheld the finality of administrative determinations, where administrative tribunals have been given jurisdiction by law, believing that the requirements of due process of law called simply for a fair trial, and not necessarily for a trial before a court of law.

The idea that a court must not reverse itself is repudiated, in many of his decisions. While, as has been remarked, he does not advocate the change of front at will by the court on all constitutional matters, yet, he believes that a decision by any court in a matter of private law vests no constitutional rights in the people which require that court to hold to the doctrine of the decision in subsequent cases.

In Massachusetts, Justice Holmes had taken occasion to approve the decision in Hurtado vs. California, and to state that no one had a vested interest in a given procedure. He found opportunity to deny this doctrine in regard to property rights in several cases before the Supreme Court. When the Court of Appeals of New York had virtually reversed a long line of its own decisions, the majority of the Supreme Court held that this reversal was an impairment of the obligation of contracts, and hence invalid. The plaintiff in error had acquired property under the law as expounded in the reversed decisions, and the overthrow of that law impaired the " contract as expressed in those cases."

Justice Holmes could not agree with this view of the rigidity of precedent, this limiting of the present by the past. He said in dissent:

In other words, we are asked to extend to the present case the principle of Gelpecke vs. Dubuque, 1 Wall. 175, . . . as to public bonds bought on the faith of a decision that they were constitutionally issued. That seems to me a great, unwarranted, and undesirable extension of a doctrine which it took this court a good while to explain. The doctrine now is explained, however, not to mean that a change in the decision impairs the obligation of contracts (Burgess vs. Seligman, 107 U. S., 20, 34) and certainly never has been supposed to mean that all property owners in a state have a vested right that no general proposition of law shall be reversed, changed, or modified by the courts if the consequences to them will be more or less pecuniary loss. I know of no constitutional principle to prevent the complete reversal of the Elevated Railroad Cases tomorrow if it should seem proper to the court of appeals.[15]

When the argument for a plaintiff in error, who had been fined for contempt of court, was that the state court had reversed a long line of decisions in order to convict him, Justice Holmes said: " There is no constitutional right to have all general propositions of law once adopted remain unchanged. Even if it be true, as the plaintiff in error says, that the supreme court of Colorado departed from earlier and well-established precedents to meet the exigencies of this case, whatever might be thought of the justice or wisdom of such a step, the Constitution of the United States is not infringed." [16]

With characteristic frankness, Justice Holmes admits that the courts may legislate. Whether they will exercise this power depends upon the necessities of the moment. If they deem it important for the administration of justice, judges may make and change law, says Justice Holmes. Obviously, he qualifies his statement, but the admission of the power in so many words is not usually found in the opinions of other judges.

A plaintiff in Massachusetts had established a prima facie case, and had then refused to produce further evidence. The

---

[15] Muhlker vs. New York and H. R. R. Co., 197 U. S., 544, J. Holmes dissenting, 571.

[16] Patterson vs. Colorado, 205 U. S., 454.

question was: Could the court order him to produce such evidence? Justice Holmes showed that neither common law nor chancery courts in England had ever made such an order, and went on to discuss the propriety of establishing such a precedent:

> We do not forget the continuous process of developing the law that goes on through the courts, in the form of deduction, or deny that in a clear case it might be possible even to break away from a line of decisions in favor of some rule generally admitted to be based upon a deeper insight into the present needs of society. . . . In the present case we perceive no such pressing need of our anticipating the legislature as to justify our departure from what we cannot doubt is the settled tradition of the common law. . . . It will be seen that we put our decision, not upon the impolicy of admitting such a power, but on the ground that it would be too great a step of judicial legislation to be justified by the necessities of the case.[17]

From Justice Holmes' works, there emerges a clear conception of the law. Private law is the changeable, living body of rules, which must be kept fresh and vigorous, whose guardianship is divided between the courts and the legislatures. Constitutional law partakes of some of the characteristics of private law, but in other respects it is sacred. Certain principles of eternal meaning have been embodied in it. It is the duty of the courts to use every means to find them out, and to preserve them inviolate. On the other hand the Constitution contains certain general and mutable provisions, which are not to be confused with the rigid and unchangeable. To separate one kind from the other, it is the duty of the courts to inquire what was meant in the first place. If the meaning was specific at its inception, it remains

---

[17] Stack vs. N. Y., N. H. & H. R. R. Co., 177 Mass., 155. The following from The Common Law, p. 78, though not directly concerned with judicial legislation, gives a hint of the attitude which Justice Holmes believes right for the courts to assume:
" The philosophical habit of the day, the frequency of legislation, and the ease with which the law may be changed to meet the opinions and wishes of the public, all make it natural and unavoidable that judges as well as others should openly discuss the legislative principles upon which their decisions must always rest in the end, and should base their judgments upon broad considerations of policy to which the tradition of the bench would hardly have tolerated a reference fifty years ago."

specific. If it was general, and capable of no definition, the proper function of the courts is to expand and develop it in the light of new necessities. The essential point of Justice Holmes' opinions is that the provisions for which a specific meaning can be found, by historical or analytical methods, must not be warped and changed by doctrinaire and scholastic interpretations. When a provision is found in the Constitution or in its amendments, and the reasons for its being there can be ascertained with accuracy, it is the duty of the courts to maintain this meaning against plausible arguments which would destroy it and substitute a significance totally antithetical to the original.

The way in which Justice Holmes believes Constitutional provisions should be interpreted when their original meaning can be discovered, is brought out clearly in his opinion dissenting from the recent decision of the court that stock dividends are not income under the 16th Amendment:

> I think that the word "incomes" in the 16th Amendment should be read in "a sense most obvious to the common understanding at the time of its adoption." Bishop vs. State, 149 Ind., 223, 230. . . . For it was for public adoption that it was proposed. M'Culloch vs. Maryland, 4 Wheat., 316, 407. . . . The known purpose of this amendment was to get rid of nice questions, as to what might be direct taxes, and I cannot doubt that most people not lawyers would suppose when they voted for it that they put a question like the present to rest.[18]

---

[18] Eisner vs. Macomber, decided March 8, 1920, J. Holmes dissenting.

# CHAPTER II

## THE LAW AND SOCIAL REFORM

The fundamental antagonism found in questions involving the change of law to conform with novel social conditions is not between two legal ideas, but between two schools of political philosophy. The struggle in every case, whether involving the common law or the Constitution, is between individualism and what Dicey calls Collectivism. Expressed in legal terms, crystallized out of the realm of theory, the problem is one of defining " liberty of contract."

Starting from the extreme individual liberty of contract preached by Bentham, and Spencer, the common law of England has undergone a practical revolution, as the police powers of the government have encroached more and more upon this liberty, in the Factory Acts, the Trade Union Acts, and the Workmen's Compensation laws. In the United States the struggle has been complicated by the limitations, express or implied, imposed by the Constitution upon the courts and legislatures. Nevertheless, the problem here has been, in essence, identical with that in England. The hitherto existing common law and Constitutional law has been interpreted in greater or less conformity with the individualism of Bentham, and this interpretation has come into conflict with the stern realities of the present, represented by the police power, ever eager for the reform of the law.

Any discussion of the opinions of Justice Holmes dealing with social reform must be inadequate to describe the place which they hold in the whole body of his works; and it will be, necessarily, open to the criticism that a false emphasis has been laid upon these, to the neglect of other opinions of possibly greater value.

Yet, there is no doubt that his dissents in the Lochner, Adair and similar cases are more widely known than any of his more technical opinions; and that he is more generally recognized as the most distinguished liberal of the American

bench than as an equally distinguished expounder of the law
of torts.

His contribution to the mass of legal opinion anent social
reform falls roughly into two classes, namely: the evolution
of the common law which he regards as necessary to meet
changing social demands, and the expansion of the state and
Federal police powers to a point where they may regulate
substantially any conditions of society which the legislative
branch of the government may find it desirable, for the good
of the community, to adjust.

In the first class, he has urged the courts to determine
considerations of social advantage when applying the common
law in doubtful cases, and to expand the accepted interpretation, if necessary, to meet the new social conditions which
have arisen since the interpretation became fixed.

In the second class, he has endeavored to limit the authority of the courts to declare unconstitutional statutes
passed ostensibly under the police power,—by adding to the
ends for which the police power may be used the sweeping
category,—general considerations of social advantage.  He
would, of course, not permit state action under the police
power, or Congressional legislation under the Commerce
Clause or the taxing power to violate any express or implied
constitutional prohibition.

But, in his interpretation of the term "constitutional prohibition," he has, on occasion, differed from the majority of
his colleagues,  Briefly, the main point of difference may
be stated thus,—that Justice Holmes gives to legislative judgment in social reform a dignity and weight above that ac-
corded it by the precedents of constitutional decisions; and
that he disregards "liberty of contract" in the extreme sense
in which it has been applied by the courts to social laws.

In "The Common Law," Justice Holmes said somewhere
that the law drew the "juices of life" from "considerations
of what is expedient to the community concerned."  We have
noted above his general views as to the functions of the

court and of the legislature in making articulate these considerations today. A discussion of his opinions on every
kind of social legislation cannot be undertaken in this paper.
The same considerations have moved him in upholding many
extensions of the police power, but they are best emphasized
by an examination of the way in which he has worked them
out and applied them in the common law and in the legislation affecting labor.

Vegelahn vs. Guntner [1] is the logical beginning of a consideration of Justice Holmes' social opinions. The facts
concern a preliminary injunction, issued by Justice Holmes,
forbidding certain acts and threats of violence during a
strike, but permitting " peaceful picketting." The majority
of the court enjoined such picketting, holding it to be one
of the means of intimidation employed by the strikers, and
therefore illegal. Justice Holmes, in his dissent, put to one
side the matter of the patrol, and went to the heart of the
question at issue, which was the social problem of the means
permitted to a labor union in carrying on its collective bargaining with employers:

The true grounds of decision are considerations of policy and of
social advantage, and it is vain to suppose that solutions can be
attained merely by logic and the general propositions of law which
nobody disputes. Propositions as to public policy rarely are unanimously accepted, and still more rarely, if ever, are capable of unan-
swerable proof. They require a special training to enable any one
even to form an intelligent opinion about them. In the early stages
of law, at least, they generally are acted on rather as inarticulate
instincts than as definite ideas for which a rational defense is ready.

There are certain grounds upon which the infliction of
temporal damages is permitted by the law. The question in
such cases as these is generally what amounts to justification. The undisputed fact that one man may deliberately
set up a business in order to ruin a rival in trade, shows
that it is permitted to interfere directly with another's welfare if it is in the course of the battle of trade.

This is on the principle that free competition is worth

---

[1] 167 Mass. 92. J. Holmes dissenting.

what it costs. Force may not be used, but an employer may persuade a man to leave one shop to take work in another. Also, he may withdraw certain financial advantages from a third party who continues to deal with a rival. If he may do these things, he may threaten to do them, for a threat is not per se unlawful. If the act threatened is privileged, the threat to do that act is privileged. Such are the acts which rivals in trade may do, in the privileged name of " free competition." " I have seen the suggestion made that the conflict between employers and employed is not competition. . . . If the policy on which our law is founded is too narrowly expressed in the term free competition, we may substitute free struggle for life. Certainly the policy is not limited to struggles between persons of the same class competing for the same end. It applies to all conflicts of temporal interests."

Thus, the Justice establishes the privileges permitted to parties engaged in free competition, and classifies labor and capital disputes as among those in which such competition is allowed.

> But there is a notion which latterly has been insisted on a good deal, that a combination of persons to do what anyone of them lawfully might do by himself will make the otherwise lawful conduct unlawful. It would be rash to say that some as yet unformulated truth may not be hidden under this proposition. But in the general form in which it has been presented and accepted by many courts, I think it plainly untrue. both on authority and on principle. . . . It is plain from the slightest consideration of practical affairs, or the most superficial reading of industrial history, that free competition means combination, and that the organization of the world, now going on so fast, means an ever increasing might and scope of combination. It seems to me futile to set our faces against this tendency. Whether beneficial on the whole, as I think it, or detrimental, it is inevitable, unless the fundamental axioms of society, and even the fundamental conditions of life, are to be changed.

By this reasoning a combination of labor is privileged to compete by the same means as a combination of capital, that is, " by argument, persuasion and the bestowal or refusal of those advantages which they otherwise lawfully control."

The legality of the secondary boycott next came before

Justice Holmes for decision. With qualifications which will be noticed shortly, he held such a boycott to be legal, thus assuming a position contrary to that of the great majority of the courts of the United States.

The primary boycott,—the refusal of an individual or group to deal with a person with whom he or they are in controversy,—is generally considered legal.

The secondary boycott, however, involving a refusal to deal with third parties who deal with the object of the primary boycott, is almost universally condemned as a malicious action, not to be justified.

In Plant vs. Woods [2] the boycott as a weapon of organized labor, if used under conditions where it would be lawful for one man to use it, without its sole motive being malice, as a means to an end lawful in itself, is sustained by Justice Holmes. Further he extends the idea of a legitimate end to the gathering of the forces of labor preliminary to the fray.

Rival labor unions were engaged in a fight for position among themselves. One of them threatened an employer with a boycott unless men of the rival union were discharged. The majority of the court granted an injunction against this boycott and against threats to the employer's business, holding that there was here no dispute between capital and labor concerning wages, but a quarrel between two elements of labor, which attacked the contractual liberty of others. They held further that the right to contract freely for one's labor is a legal right, and entitled to legal protection.

The motive here was taken as malicious. The majority opinion specifically refused to recognize Allen vs. Flood,[3] a then recent English case that in somewhat similar facts decided that a malicious motive did not per se make otherwise legal action liable in a civil suit, if the statements made with this motive were justified by the end desired in making them.

Justice Holmes, dissenting, asserted that the actions of

---

[2] 176 Mass. 492, J. Holmes dissenting.
[3] 1898 Appeal Cases (Gt. Britain), 1.

the union were justified, even though there was no current
dispute about wages. The fact that the end to which the
threats were made was a strengthening of the union, in order
that it might present a more formidable front in the subsequent disputes which were its reason for existing, he held to
be a justification for actions which he had intimated to be
lawful, in a wages dispute in Vegelahn vs. Guntner.

Justice Holmes amply qualifies his assertion of the legality
of the boycott, as has been noted above: " I infer that a
majority of my brethren would admit that a boycott or strike
intended to raise wages directly might be lawful, if it did
not embrace in its scheme or intent violence, breach of contract, or other conduct unlawful on grounds independent of
the mere fact that the action of the defendants was com-
bined." He goes on to state his belief in the justification
present in this case:

> That purpose (of the present boycott) was not directly concerned
> with wages. It was one degree more remote. The immediate object
> and motive was to strengthen the defendants' society as a prelimi-
> nary and means to enable it to make a better fight on questions of
> wages or other matters of clashing interests. I differ from my
> brethren in thinking that the threats were as lawful for this pre-
> liminary purpose as for the final one to which strengthening the
> union was a means. I think that unity of organization is necessary
> to make the contest of labor effectual, and that societies of laborers
> lawfully may employ in their preparation the means which they
> might use in the final contest.

In conclusion he disavows any serious belief in the universal social benefits to be obtained from the organization
of labor, for he finds that there is only so much to be had
of the world's goods, and if one group of laborers by organization gets more than its share, it does so at the expense of
some other group not so well equipped for bargaining. " But,
subject to the qualifications which I have expressed, I think
it lawful for a body of workmen to try by combination to
get more than they now are getting, although they do it at
the expense of their fellows, and to that end to strengthen
their union by the boycott and by the strike."

The advance from his dictum in Vegelahn vs. Guntner

is twofold: (1) that the strengthening of a labor union is a proper justification for an act which is otherwise actionable; (2) that, consequently, a boycott of the nature specified here, is a lawful weapon of organized labor under these circumstances.

It is in point here to note that Justice Holmes concurs in a recent dissent in the Hitchman case, 245 U. S. 259, from the court's opinion granting an injunction to forbid labor organizers operating in a mine where the contract of employment stipulated that the laborers would not join a labor union. The organizers had been persuading workmen to leave employment until the owners would agree to unionization. The court held this to be a malicious interference. Justices Brandeis and Holmes believed the end justified the means.

It goes without saying that Justice Holmes does not wish to open the door to a freedom of action on the part of labor that will defy liability for unlawful acts. The acts of labor unions heretofore considered are privileged by him only when done for justifiable ends.

When no justification existed, he has applied the law as sternly to labor unions as to individuals. In the case of May vs. Wood,[4] there was involved an action in tort, to recover damages from the defendants for conspiring together to induce one Mary A. Wood to break a contract of labor.

The defendant demurred to the declaration on the ground that it did not "set out the words or the substance of the words of the false and malicious statements which said William Wood is alleged to have conspired to make."

The demurrer was sustained in the lower court, and by the majority of the Supreme Judicial Court. It was held that such alleged malicious statements must be set out on the face of the declaration.

Justice Holmes dissented, believing the pleadings sufficient, and believing that the case should have been heard on the

---

[4] 172 Mass., 11, J. Holmes dissenting, 14.

merits: "I regard it as settled in this Commonwealth, and as rightly settled, whether it be consistent with some dicta of Allen vs. Flood (1898) A. C., 1, or not, that an action will lie for depriving a man of custom, that is, of possible contracts, as well when the result is effected by persuasion as when it is accomplished by fraud or force, if the harm is inflicted simply from malevolence and without some justifiable cause, such as competition in trade."

Similarly, in Moran vs. Dunphy,[5] he held an inducement to breach of contract unlawful, where the facts showed none of the justifications which he had enumerated in the cases previously considered.

The first case involving labor legislation in which Justice Holmes expressed himself after becoming a member of the Supreme Court of the United States was Lochner vs. New York.[6] The dissenting opinion which he delivered has become classic. It expounds fully his point of view towards social legislation, and its constitutionality. Moreover, it lays the foundation for his subsequent dissents, which work out more in detail, but do not alter, the doctrine set forth in this case.

The New York law limiting work in bakeries to ten hours daily was held unconstitutional, the court differentiating it from the law upheld in Holden vs. Hardy[7] on the ground that it was not a matter of "common understanding" that more than ten hours of work in a bakery was unhealthy, while in the case of Holden vs. Hardy it had been shown that an eight hour law for miners was necessary as a health measure.

The necessary implication of this decision was that the judgment of a state legislature as to the necessity of an alleged health law was not final, but that the necessity of all such laws must be proved affirmatively to the Supreme Court. Failing such proof, the Supreme Court, having no

[5] 177 Mass., 485. See also Western vs. Barnicoat, 175 Mass., 454.
[6] 198 U. S., 45, J. Holmes dissenting, 74.
[7] 169 U. S., 366, upholding Colorado 8 hour law for miners, where the danger of the occupation was recognized by "common understanding."

knowledge of local conditions other than what was shown in
the testimony, which does not appear to have been of a statistical or expert nature, will declare the state law unconstitutional as beyond the police power of the state, infringing the
liberty of contract guaranteed by the 14th Amendment.

The term "common understanding" seems to be taken
to mean, in this decision, the understanding of the court,
rather than of the legislature, or of the general public opinion
of the state. Furthermore, the court laid stress on the fact
that employees in bakeries were not suffering from any dis-
abilities, were not wards of the state, and thus were free to
make any sort of a contract of labor that they chose.

Here the extreme individualistic interpretation of the 14th
Amendment was given by the majority, in direct antithesis
to the principle which Justice Holmes believed appropriate
to this case. The court placed the burden of proof upon the
legislature; Justice Holmes placed it upon the court. The
fact that the legislature had seen fit to pass the law was proof
to Justice Holmes that the law was what it purported to
be according to the "common understanding." It then could
only be held unconstitutional if no "reasonable man" might
say that it would accomplish what the legislature intended.

He first cited examples of interference by law with the
liberty of contract, notably the Sunday laws, usury laws, and
lottery laws: "The liberty of the citizen to do as he likes
so long as he does not interfere with the liberty of others
to do the same, which has been a shibboleth for some well-
known writers, is interfered with by school laws, by the Post-
office, by every state or municipal institution which takes
his money for purposes thought desirable, whether he likes
it or not." Prohibitions of combinations by law are familiar,[8]
sale of stock on margin has been forbidden by California,[9]
and an eight hour law for miners has been upheld.[10] "The
14th Amendment does not enact Mr. Herbert Spencer's Social Statics." Nor did it enact any particular economic

---

[8] Northern Securities Case, 193 U. S., 197.
[9] Otis vs. Parker, 187 U. S., 606.
[10] Holden vs. Hardy, 169 U. S., 366.

theory, either of paternalism or of laissez faire. The legislative judgment is to be taken as final, since a reasonable man might uphold the law as a health measure or " as a first installment of a general regulation of the hours of work."

This opinion repudiates the doctrine of liberty of contract as applying to relations between employer and employee. With this impediment out of the way, Justice Holmes' view is certain of success. Indeed, the impossibility of the attitude of the majority came to be recognized by the court, and, though hesitatingly, it has allowed a gradual broadening of the police power until, in the recent case of Bunting vs. Oregon,[11] an hours of labor law applying to adult males in occupations not at all dangerous was sustained—though the ostensible basis of the decision was the necessity of the law as a health measure, shown by the statistical brief prepared by the present Justice Brandeis and Mr. Felix Frankfurter.

First, then, in Massachusetts, Justice Holmes sought wider common law rights for the labor organization in its encounters with the employer. Next, on the Supreme Court, he placed within the police power of the state the regulation of the hours of labor contract between employer and employee. Finally, he upheld a virtual combination of the two principles in attempts by the Federal and state governments to give affirmative protection to the labor union, and to regulate the contracts of labor at the same time.

It will thus be seen that he recognizes that there is an intrinsic inequality between the positions of " capital " and "labor," and believes it compatible with the police power for the legislature to decide that this inequality should be remedied by law, for the general welfare of the community. The fictitious equality between the employer and employee has been maintained by the extreme interpretation of " freedom of contract" which generally American courts have given. The maintenance of this fiction has in fact produced an inequality.[12]

---

[11] 243 U. S., 426.
[12] Roscoe Pound, Yale Law Rev., 454.

Without expressing his personal approval or disapproval of existing industrial conditions, Justice Holmes believes that the workman actually needs the paternal care of the state to a certain extent in his bargaining, as has been shown by the laws of States and of Congress which attempt to give this protection. The fact that the majority legislative opinion is to this effect,—evidenced by the legislation,—makes the object desired a legitimate one within the police power, for the reasonable man cannot say that it will not be to the advantage of society.

The power of the Federal Government is to be derived from the regulatory power exercised under the Commerce Clause; that of the States, of course, is the police power which permits them to legislate for the moral and physical good of their people. " In present conditions a workman not unnaturally may believe that only by belonging to a union can he secure a contract that shall be fair to him. . . . If that belief, whether right or wrong, may be held by a reasonable man, it seems to me that it may be enforced by law in order to establish the equality of position between the parties in which liberty of contract begins." [13]

The majority of the Supreme Court in Adair vs. United States,[14] held that so much of the Erdman Law, a Federal Statute, as forbade the discharge of an employee of an interstate carrier on account of his membership in a labor union, was unconstitutional as impairing the liberty of contract interpreted to be guaranteed by the 5th Amendment. Many States have enacted legislation similar to the Erdman Act, and such legislation has been uniformly held unconstitutional by State Tribunals.[15] It further held that there was no such connection between membership in a labor union and interstate commerce as gave Congress authority to legislate under the Commerce Clause. Justice Harlan made the statement that " in all such particulars the employer and the em-

---

[13] Coppage vs. Kansas, 236 U. S., 1, J. Holmes dissenting, 26.
[14] 208 U. S., 168, J. Holmes dissenting, 190.
[15] Commons and Andrews, Principles of Labor Legislation, p. 113.

ployee have equality of right, and any legislation that disturbs that equality is an arbitrary interference with the liberty of contract which no government can legally justify in a free land."

Justice Holmes, in his dissent, argues that labor unions are closely enough connected with interstate commerce to be subject to Congressional regulations; but he bases his chief criticism of the decision upon social grounds. He finds the law to be a very limited interference with liberty of contract:

> I confess that I think that the right to make contracts at will that has been derived from the word 'liberty' in the Amendments has been stretched to its extreme by the decisions; but they agree that sometimes the right may be restrained. Where there is, or generally is believed to be, an important ground of public policy for restraint, the Constitution does not forbid it, whether this court agrees or disagrees with the policy pursued. It cannot be doubted that to prevent strikes, and, so far as possible, to foster its scheme of arbitration, might be deemed by Congress to be an important point of policy, and I think it impossible to say that Congress might not reasonably think that the provision in question would help a good deal to carry its policy along.
> But suppose the only effect really were to tend to bring about the complete unionizing of such railroad laborers as Congress can deal with, I think that object alone would justify the act.

So, in the Lochner and the Adair cases Justice Holmes has attempted to add two new areas for the exercise of the police power—" a general regulation of the hours of work," and " the complete unionizing of such railroad laborers as Congress can deal with." The statements themselves show more clearly than could any comment the differences between Justice Holmes' views and the long line of decisions of the Supreme Court enshrining " liberty of contract " in a hallowed niche among the fundamental guarantees of the Constitution.

In Coppage vs. Kansas, a Kansas law was held unconstitutional which forbade prescribing as a condition precedent to employment that the employee would not join a labor union during employment. The grounds of the decision were substantially the same as those in the Adair case. Justice Holmes' concise dissenting opinion cites the dissents in Massa-

chusetts and in the Supreme Court, and affirms his belief
that the principles which he expressed in them apply equally
well to the case in question. Concluding, he says: " Whether
in the long run it is wise for the workingmen to enact legislation of this sort is not my concern, but I am strongly of
opinion that there is nothing in the Constitution of the United
States to prevent it, and that Adair vs. U. S. . . . and Lochner vs. N. Y. . . . should be overruled."

In a Massachusetts case, decided in 1891,[16] Holmes sustained the constitutionality of a state law prohibiting the
imposition of fines upon workmen by employers on account
of imperfect work. The majority of the court held that this
was an interference with the liberty of contract, and hence
unconstitutional. Justice Holmes, dissenting, stated clearly
his opinion that the legislative judgment was binding, where
no clear proof of its error was presented to the court.[17]

That the legislature may regulate the method of payment
of wages is the opinion of the Supreme Judicial Court of
Massachusetts, to which Justice Holmes subscribed.[18] It is
difficult to reconcile this opinion with the avowed " freedom
of contract " beliefs of the Massachusetts court. However,
it is in accord with the view of the United States Supreme
Court.[19]

The argument presented in the opinion of the Justices
approaches very closely to Justice Holmes' reasoning in Lochner vs. New York. " Freedom of contract " is not found in
the Massachusetts Bill of Rights specifically. Economic the-

---

[16] Commonwealth vs. Perry, 155 Mass., 117, J. Holmes dissenting,
123.

[17] " I suppose that this act was passed because the operatives or
some of them, thought that they often were cheated out of a part
of their wages under a false pretense that the work done by them
was imperfect, and persuaded the Legislature that their view was
true.

" If their view was true, I cannot doubt that the Legislature
could deprive the employers of an honest tool, which they were
using for a dishonest purpose, and I cannot pronounce the legislation void, as based on a false assumption, since I know nothing
about the matter one way or the other."

[18] Opinion of the Justices, 163 Mass., 589 (1895).

[19] See Knoxville Iron Co. vs. Harbison, 183 U. S., 13; McLean vs.
Arkansas, 211 U. S., 539.

ories have changed since the adoption of the Bill. There are
certain well-known restrictions on the freedom of contract.
The decision of the Legislature in this matter is based on
public policy, and the courts can only inquire if it is plainly
repugnant to the Constitution. There has been similar legislation in foreign countries and in some of the States. Therefore, " we cannot say, as a matter of law, that the legislation
proposed is so plainly not wholesome, or reasonable, that the
General Court may not judge it to be for the good and welfare
of the Commonwealth."

Justice Holmes has not delivered the opinion of the Court
in any one of the recent cases sustaining Workmen's Compensation and Employers' Liability Laws. However, he has been
found always on the side of their constitutionality,—a position that was to be expected of him. Concurring, in the
Arizona Employees' Liability Case,[20] he says: " There is some
argument made for the general proposition that immunity
from liability when not in fault is a right inherent in free
government. . . . But if it is thought to be public policy
to put certain voluntary conduct at the peril of those pur-
suing it whether in the interest of safety or upon economic
or other grounds, I know of nothing to hinder."

When the Supreme Court declared the first Federal Employers' Liability Law unconstitutional on the ground that
its words applied to acts not under the authority given to
Congress by the Commerce Clause, Justice Holmes believed
that it was possible to save the constitutionality of the law
"without doing violence to the habits of English speech,"
by narrowing the words by the interpretation put on them.[21]
Certainly the suggested interpretation would have saved the
necessity for redrafting the law and for its second passage
by Congress. Considerations of public policy were with Justice Holmes in this case.[22]

---

[20] Arizona Copper Co. vs. Hammer, Dec. June 9, 1919, J. Holmes
concurring.

[21] Howard vs. Illinois Central R. R. Co., 207 U. S., 463, J. Holmes
dissenting, 541.

[22] See J. H. Ralston, " Judicial Control Over Legislatures," in 54
American Law Rev., 1, 32.

Justice Holmes came to the bench in 1882, when the transition from individualism to collectivism in England was in progress. Throughout his career on the Supreme Judicial Court of Massachusetts, the English law was being amended by socialistic legislation. Before he was called to Washington, the change in the labor code of England was complete in its essential respects. Justice Holmes was too learned in the history of the law to be blind to the fact that the socialistic trend in American political thought would finally demand extensive paternal legislation in no uncertain terms; and that when this demand became strong enough serious consequences might follow the failure of the courts to acquiesce in the legislative program.

The supremacy of Parliament had made easy the introduction of new ideas into the English law. But the control of the legislature by American courts raised a serious obstacle to the crystallization of opinion into law which the courts would hold constitutional. Yet, the necessity for the establishment of a benevolent attitude towards social reform was apparent to Justice Holmes. At the time when he was first stating his views, the Constitution was regarded as almost immutable. Amendment had come only as the result of civil war, and, to many commentators, no further change might be looked for short of a popular upheaval.[23]

Next to amendment of the Constitution, the most feasible means of giving validity to new principles was to change the interpretation of the provisions under which the inevitable social legislation would be held invalid. " Liberty of contract " and the broad powers of review assumed by the courts under the 5th and 14th Amendments were the elements which barred the way to reform,—and it is against these interpretations that Justice Holmes' most significant attacks have been directed.

The views of constitutional interpretation here attributed to Justice Holmes might be thought to be the reflections of his personal beliefs in something akin to socialism. But

---

[23] Bryce, American Commonwealth, chap. xxxi.

the contrary is true. To state his economic ideas affirmatively is not easy, but he has plainly indicated the things in which he does not believe. Curiously, they are the same things for which he has most stubbornly sought legal recognition when they were demanded by public opinion. He continually warns the courts against allowing personal views to cloud their judgment. He would not have the court attempt to mould public opinion, but, after opinion had crystallized into law, he would have the court make it effective.

In his judicial opinions, in his legal essays, and in his speeches, Justice Holmes has maintained this idea; but at the same time he has disavowed his belief in socialism, and has refused to affirm his confidence in paternalism, or in any great benefits which may come from the complete organization of labor.

I believe that the wholesale social regeneration which so many now seem to expect, if it can be helped by conscious, co-ordinated human effort, cannot be affected appreciably by tinkering with the institution of property, but only by taking in hand life and trying to build a new race. That would be my starting point for an ideal for the law. The notion that with socialized property we should have women free and a piano for everybody seems to me an empty humbug.[24]

I have no belief in panaceas and almost none in sudden ruin. . . . Hence I am not much interested one way or the other in the nostrums now so strenuously urged.[25]

This case is decided upon an economic theory which a large part of the country does not entertain. If it were a question whether I agreed with that theory, I should desire to study it further and long before making up my mind.[26]

I think it well to add that I cherish no illusions as to the meaning and effect of strikes. While I think the strike a lawful instrument in the universal struggle of life, I think it pure phantasy to suppose that there is a body of capital of which labor as a whole secures a larger share by that means.[27]

These statements show pretty conclusively that Justice Holmes is not fired with a socialistic ardor. He emphasizes, however, the social basis which is the ultimate foundation of the law. " The time has gone by," said Justice Holmes twen-

[24] Ideals and Doubts, Ill. Law Review, May, 1915, p. 1, 3.
[25] Law and the Court, 1913, Speeches, p. 98.
[26] Lochner vs. New York, 176 Mass., 492, J. Holmes dissenting.
[27] Plant vs. Woods, 176 Mass., 492, J. Holmes dissenting.

ty-six years ago, " when law is only an unconscious embodiment of the common will. It has become a conscious reaction
upon itself of organized society knowingly seeking to determine its own destinies." [28]   And again:

Everyone instinctively recognizes that in these days the justification of a law for us cannot be found in the fact that our fathers
always have followed it.  It must be found in some help which the
law brings toward reaching a social end which the governing power
of the community has made up its mind that it wants.[29]

But inasmuch as the real justification of a rule of law, if there
be one, is that it helps to bring about a social end which we desire,
it is no less necessary that those who make and develop the law
should have those ends articulately in their minds.[30]

That this fundamental social basis of the law has been lost
sight of by the courts is Justice Holmes' belief.[31]   In his
earliest legal writings he recognized the social sources of the
law,[32] and he has never abandoned this conception in his
consideration of new and seemingly revolutionary statutes
striking at the roots of the established social order.

His liberality towards the novel in legislation is predicated
upon the conviction that the social theories of no period have
been written or properly interpreted into the fundamental
law of the land; that " a constitution is not intended to em-
body a particular economic theory "; and that, consequently,
social ideas which have been accepted by the courts and have
come by usage to be conceived of as a part of the organic
law and immutable, are not in reality of any greater weight
than other and newer social beliefs.  Therefore, he argues, it
is the duty of the courts to note the change in the very nature
of society, and to do away with the theories of the past that
are erroneously being applied to the present.[33]

The reaction against socialistic preachings, when they first
were heard by the country, led to an almost universal accept-

---

[28] Privilege, Malice and Intent, 8 Harv. Law Rev., 1, 9.
[29] Law in Science and Science in Law, 12 Harv. Law Rev., 443, 452.
[30] Ibid., 460.
[31] Thus, he says: " I think that the judges themselves have failed
adequately to recognize their duty of weighing considerations of
social advantage " (Path of the Law, 10 Harv. Law Rev., 457, 467).
[32] See early pages of The Common Law.
[33] Lochner vs. New York, 198 U. S., 45.

ance by courts of the economic view of Adam Smith and the legal philosophy of Bentham.[34]   The doctrine of laissez faire was interpreted into the guarantes of liberty in the Bill of Rights and in the 14th Amendment, and out of this grew the "freedom of contract" which has consistently blocked the way to social reform.

When socialism first began to be talked about, the comfortable classes of the community were a good deal frightened. I suspect that this fear has influenced judicial action both here and in England. . . . I think that something similar led people who no longer hope to control the legislatures to look to the courts as expounders of the Constitutions, and that in some courts new principles have been discovered outside the bodies of those instruments, which may be generalized into acceptance of the economic doctrines which prevailed about fifty years ago, and a wholesale prohibition of what a tribunal of lawyers does not think about right.[35]

The tenacity with which the courts have held to these doctrines as fixed constitutional principles, Justice Holmes does not find surprising. "No doubt the history of the law encourages scepticism when one sees how far a rule or a doctrine has grown up, or when one notices the naivete with which social prejudices are taken for eternal principles. But it also leads to an unconvinced conservatism." [36]

This conservatism is to be expected of courts on account of the habits of thought which are natural to judges, who, "especially as they grow older, resent attempts to push analysis beyond consecrated phrases, or to formulate anew." [37]

Justice Holmes does not wholly condemn conservatism.

---

[34] Liberty of Contract, by Roscoe Pound, 18 Yale Law Rev., 454, discusses the development of this theory. The first American statement of it appears in Godcharles vs. Wigeman, 113 Pa. St., 431.   It was a logical consequence of the individualism preached by Bentham and Mill, superimposed upon the natural rights political philosophy in which the American Constitution was founded.

[35] Path of the Law, 10 Harv. Law Rev., p. 467.

[36] Review of "Holdsworth's English Law," in Law Quarterly Review, Oct. 1909, 412, 414.

[37] Answer to Resolutions, on Wm. Allen, Speeches, p. 52.   This idea is also expressed in the following from "Privilege, Malice and Intent": "Perhaps one of the reasons why judges do not like to discuss questions of policy, or to put a decision in terms upon their views as lawmakers, is that the moment you leave the path of merely logical deduction you lose the illusion of certainty which makes legal reasoning seem like mathematics."

He would not lightly overrule precedents. However, when there comes a doubtful case he points out that the struggle is between two social desires, and that the decision rests upon the choice of the judge.[88] When the judge is called upon to exercise this prerogative of choice in a case involving an attempt to change the social status quo, the fact of the novelty of the idea is not an argument against it, and must not influence the judgment.

[A Constitution] is made for people of fundamentally differing views, and the accident of our finding certain opinions natural and familiar, or novel, and even shocking, ought not to conclude our judgment upon the question whether statutes embodying them conflict with the Constitution of the United States.

General propositions do not decide concrete cases. The decision will depend on a judgment or intuition more subtle than any articulate major premise. But I think that the proposition just stated, if it is accepted, will carry us far toward the end. Every opinion tends to become a law. I think that the word "liberty," in the 14th Amendment, is perverted when it is held to prevent the natural outcome of a dominant opinion, unless it can be said that a rational and fair man necessarily would admit that the statute proposed would infringe fundamental principles as they have been understood by the traditions of our people and our law.[89]

By the criterion established is this statement, Justice Holmes denies that principles based on the laissez faire theories of the 19th Century English economists would be judged by his "rational and fair man" to be any part of our fundamental law. Therefore, they are not to be held as binding in the judicial consideration of social questions as they arise today.

In such cases the legislative body is the judge of the advisability of a social reform. Its decision finally disposes of the question of social advantage. The judge is concerned only with the constitutionality of the measure. He must not let his own prejudice lead him to pronounce for or against a particular economic theory. He is to decide simply: Is this measure a result of a majority belief that it will be for the social good of the community? He is not concerned

---

[88] Law in Science and Science in Law, 12 Harvard Law Review, 460-461.

[89] Lochner vs. New York, 198 U. S., 45.

with the question: Should the majority believe this measure to be advantageous socially? There is nothing of ethics involved. The fact of a predominant opinion as to the social advantage is sufficient justification for a law, where no indisputable constitutional guarantee is plainly infringed. " Judges are apt to be naif, simple-minded men, and they need something of Mephistopheles. We too need education in the obvious,—to learn to transcend our own convictions and to leave room for much that we hold dear to be done away with short of revolution by the orderly change of law." [40]

Justice Holmes' opinions have been vindicated in at least one direction. His attitude towards hours of labor laws has come to be that of the Supreme Court in practice, and of many inferior courts as is evidenced by recent widely scattered decisions upholding hours of labor laws.

The decisions reached by the courts in this matter have coincided with Justice Holmes' of fifteen years ago, but in the manner of courts reversing themselves, the reasoning has given no hint that the new position is in any way different from the old. Hours of labor laws are now sustained as health measures—following the development by counsel of the statistical method of presenting argument in favor of social legislation. This innovation may, without stretching the imagination too greatly, be partially credited to Justice Holmes' writings, and his influence with the section of the bar which has been instrumental in framing the statistical method of argument.

With his recognition that changing social conditions demanded new laws, Justice Holmes realized that perhaps many of these laws were too far in advance of the " common understanding" to find acceptance in the courts. While accepting the new himself on purely legal grounds, as we have seen, he suggested the necessity for a scientific determination of the worth of the new social legislation. In 1899, he said:

I have tried to show by examples something of the interest of science as applied to the law, and to point out some possible im-

---

[40] Law and the Court, 1913, Speeches, p. 98.

provement in our way of approaching practical questions in the same sphere. . . . I have in mind an ultimate dependence upon science because it is finally for science to determine, so far as it can, the relative worth of our different social ends, and, as I have tried to hint, it is our estimate of the proportion between these, now often blind and unconscious, that leads us to insist upon and to enlarge the sphere of one principle and to allow another gradually to dwindle into atrophy.

Before this time, he had made the significant predication. " For the rational study of the law the black-letter man may be the man of the present, but the man of the future is the man of statistics and the master of economics."

The means of approach devised by the present Justice Brandeis in Muller vs. Oregon and Bunting vs. Oregon, seems very closely predicted by Justice Holmes. The fact that statistics were powerful enough to convince the Supreme Court in these cases, and, in numerous other decisions, to persuade lower courts of the healthfulness of hours of labor laws, leads inevitably to the belief that a statistical argument will be formulated which will legalize the protection of labor in its equality of bargaining, and will enable the courts to abandon their present position in that regard, in fact if not in theory.

# CHAPTER III

## COMMERCE CLAUSE

The decisions concerning the powers of Congress under the Commerce Clause, in which Justice Holmes has participated, have marked out a new field for the exercise of a Federal police power—a power admittedly necessary under the industrial conditions of the past twenty years—but nevertheless a power probably far beyond the imagination of the framers of the Constitution. The regulations which have passed Congress since the beginning of the century, and the Supreme Court's interpretations of the few similar pieces of legislation already on the statute books, have resulted in a centralization in the national government of control of matters which have required a subtle reasoning to bring them into connection with interstate commerce.

In general, the Supreme Court has shown itself to be in full accord with Congressional views of public policy in these questions, and has contrived to sustain most of the legislation under what may properly be termed the Federal police power. In cases where the Court has found that Congress attempted more than the Commerce Clause could be interpreted to authorize, Justice Holmes has differed with his colleagues in several notable dissenting opinions. When the Court has sustained legislation of this nature, he has always been with the majority.

In the light of his expressed beliefs as to social legislation of all kinds, the benevolent attitude of Justice Holmes towards this extension of Congressional control is natural. It would have been inconsistent indeed for a judge who had endeavored to interpret the common law to conform to changed social conditions, and who had vehemently championed the right of a state to base its police regulations upon considerations of social advantage, to deny to Congress the power to legislate in behalf of the general good—when such legislation could be sustained conveniently under a clause of the Constitution whose possibilities had not yet been fully expounded.

48

That he has gone further, on occasion, than the majority of the court, in upholding police regulations of Congress under the Commerce Clause has been noticed before as the logical working out of his often expressed beliefs in the social justification to be permitted to the police power.

The constitutionality of the Sherman Anti-Trust Act had been settled before Justice Holmes took his seat upon the court at Washington, but the interpretation of that law was coming to be matter of vital national importance. He has filed one strong dissenting opinion in regard to the court's interpretation. But, since the Northern Securities case,[1] in 1904, he has been with the majority in applying the provisions of the law. However, his views in that case have had some practical influence, and have served to mark out pretty definitely the limits beyond which the prohibitions of the Sherman Act cannot be made to reach without danger to the industrial and financial stability of the nation.

Justice Holmes has shared none of the antipathy towards combinations per se which has been apparent in some degree since the agitation for the anti-trust acts began. In Massachusetts he repudiated the idea that the acts of a combination were illegal because of the existence of the combination. What he thought true of combinations of labor, he thought equally true of combinations of capital. Prosecution for being, and not for doing, was, to him, justified under no proper principle of the law. Hence, his liberalism is unique in that it is applied to capital as well as to labor. He believes that combinations of both have their necessary place in the general order of things, and he would no more destroy the one than the other.

The Northern Securities Company was incorporated under the laws of New Jersey, for the purpose of acquiring and holding a majority of the stock of the Great Northern and the Northern Pacific Railroads, which were parallel and competing roads. The Company was enjoined from voting this stock on the ground that the company was a combina-

---

[1] 193 U. S., 197, J. Holmes dissenting, 400.

tion in restraint of interstate trade and a monopoly, and
therefore guilty of a violation of the Sherman Anti-Trust
Act.

The opinion of the court, delivered by Justice Brewer, held
that the acquisition of the stock was an act having the effect
of restraining trade, preventing competition, and establishing
a monopoly, all contrary to the law.  No affirmative monopo-
listic or restrictive acts had been done by the company.  The
possession of the power to do them, and the probable intent
to do them, were held to justify the injunction.

Justice Holmes, who spoke also for Chief Justice Fuller
and Justices White and Peckham, after insisting upon a
strict construction of the words of a criminal statute, under-
took to show that the acts of the Company constituted neither a monopoly nor a combination in restraint of trade at
common law, and that the Act had not given any definition
of monopoly or combinaion in restraint of trade; therefore,
the common law definitions must have been meant.

A single railroad down a narrow valley or through a mountain
gorge monopolizes all the railroad transportation through that
valley or gorge.  Indeed, every railroad monopolizes, in a popular
sense, the trade of some area.

A monopoly of ' any part ' of commerce among the states is unlawful. . . . But the act of Congress will not be construed to mean
the universal disintegration of society into single men, each at war
with all the rest, or even the prevention of all further combinations
for a common end.

The common law idea of a combination in restraint of
trade required some attempt to keep competitors out of the
field.  Some affirmative act was required.  Justice Holmes
maintained that no such act had been shown in this case:
" This act is construed by the government to affect the pur-
chasers of shares in two railroad companies because of the
effect it may have, or, if you like, is certain to have, upon
the competition of these roads.  If such a remote result of
the exercise of an ordinary incident of property and personal
freedom is enough to make that exercise unlawful, there is
hardly any transaction concerning commerce between the
states that may not be made a crime by the finding of a jury
or a court."

Whatever may have been the merits of the majority opinion in this case,—and it is difficult to condemn the court's decision on grounds of public policy,—the warning sounded by Justice Holmes has apparently been of some influence. The doctrine of the majority has not been pushed to the logical extreme perceived by Justice Holmes, but has been steadily restricted.

In his dissent, Justice Holmes pointed out that the size of the combination was not to be considered under the words of the Act; that the natural inclination was to read the law as against great combinations only; but that the law said "every" and "any part" and therefore applied to the small as well as the great.

Clearly, the Sherman Act was not intended to break up the business organization of the United States, and the realization of that fact has led the Court to make a distinction in practice between the good trusts and the bad trusts of which President Roosevelt spoke. Further, the later cases have been decided on proof of affirmative illegal acts of a combination, and not on a more or less remote probability of their occurrence.

United States vs. United States Steel Corporation [2] seems to repudiate finally the principle of the majority in the Northern Securities Case that the ability to do wrong,—the possession of the power to monopolize and to restrain trade,—is in itself illegal. Justice McKenna, speaking for the majority, said: "Shall we declare the law to be that size is an offense, even though it minds its own business, because what it does is imitated? The Corporation is undoubtedly of impressive size, and it takes an effort of resolution not to be affected by it or to exaggerate its influence. But we must adhere to the law, and the law does not make mere size an offense or the existence of unexerted power an offense. It, we repeat, requires overt acts, and trusts to its prohibition of the man and its powers to repress or punish them."

Justice Holmes concurred with the majority in this deci-

---

[2] Dec. Mch. 1, 1920.

sion. While the Northern Securities Case is not mentioned by Justice McKenna, his words must be taken as overruling the doctrine set forth in it, and as fully vindicating the opinion of Justice Holmes, after seventeen years.

The acquittal of the Steel Corporation further repudiates the principle of the Northern Securities Case in view of the admission that the Corporation had been guilty of illegal acts prior to the institution of the dissolution suit in 1911, and thus demonstrated in practice its powers of monopoly and restraint of trade, while the Northern Securities Company had not performed any act per se illegal, or constituting a common law intent to monopolize or to restrain trade.[3]

However, just as he applied the common law rigorously to the unjustified acts of labor organizations in Massachusetts, so has he applied the Sherman Act to combinations of capital whose acts were illegal by the criteria which he had established.

A proved intent to restrain trade, by the standards of the common law, has seemed to Justice Holmes ample ground to enforce the Act. Thus, in a case where it was alleged that the acts contemplated would have been lawful even if done, he remarked: " It is enough to say that some of them conceivably might have been adequate to accomplish the result, and that the intent alleged would convert what on their face might be no more than ordinary acts of competition or the small dishonesties of trade into a conspiracy of wider scope, as has been explained more than once." [4]

Delivering the opinion of a unanimous court in Swift vs. United States,[5] the Beef Trust case, he brought out even more plainly the importance of the intent:

---

[3] Justice Holmes concurred in the dissent from the recent decision dissolving the Reading Railroad Coal combination. The majority opinion, of four Justices, placed a technical construction upon the Sherman Act and the Commodities Clause, apparently modifying in some respects, the doctrine of the Steel Trust Case. The division of the court was the same as in the Steel Trust case, with the exception of Justice McKenna, who joined Justices Pitney, Clark and Day (who dissented from the Steel Trust decision) to form a majority in the Reading case.

[4] Nash vs. U. S., 229 U. S., 373.

[5] 196 U. S., 375.

The statute gives this proceeding against combinations in restraint of commerce among the states and against attempts to monopolize the same. Intent is almost essential to such a combination, and is essential to such an attempt. Where acts are not sufficient in themselves to produce a result which the law seeks to prevent,—for instance, the monopoly,—but require further acts in addition to the mere forces of nature to bring that result to pass, an intent to bring it to pass is necessary in order to produce a dangerous probability that it will happen. . . . But when that intent and the consequent dangerous probability exist, this statute, like many others, and like the common law in some cases, directs itself against the dangerous probability as well as against the completed result.

In the Beef Trust Case, acts had been done which were intended to restrain trade; therefore, Justice Holmes distinguished it without difficulty from his conception of the Northern Securities Case, and agreed with the Court in applying the Sherman Act.

The Danbury Hatters[6] case did not disclose him as dissenting from the decision that labor unions were amenable to the Sherman Act, an additional example, if one were necessary, of his impartial administration of justice to labor and capital alike.

It is not within the scope of this study to examine in detail all of the cases in which the Commerce Clause has been involved since Justice Holmes came to the bench. It has been noted previously that he upheld the Erdman Act,[7] and both Federal Employers' Liability Acts.[8] Other important Congressional legislation under the Commerce Clause which he has been in agreement with the court in sustaining are: The Adamson Eight-Hour Law;[9] The Lottery Act, excluding lottery tickets from interstate commerce;[10] the Mann White Slave Act;[11] the act excluding prize fight films from interstate commerce;[12] the Pure Food Laws;[13] the

---

[6] Loewe vs. Lawlor, 208 U. S., 274.
[7] Adair vs. United States, 208 U. S., 161, J. Holmes dissenting.
[8] 207 U. S., 463, J. Holmes dissenting; 223 U. S., 1.
[9] Wilson vs. New, 243 U. S., 332.
[10] Champion vs. Ames, 188 U. S., 321.
[11] Hoke vs. United States, 227 U. S., 308.
[12] Weber vs. Freed, 239 U. S., 325.
[13] Hippolite Egg Company vs. United States, 220 U. S., 45; McDermott vs. Wisconsin, 228 U. S., 115; Hebe Co. vs. Shaw, 248 U. S., 297.

Webb-Kenyon Act;[14] the Reed "Bone-Dry" Amendment.[15]

After 1908, when the Adair case brought him into conflict with the majority of the court, Justice Holmes found no occasion to differ with his colleagues on a matter of Congressional regulation of commerce until the Federal Child Labor law came before the court in 1917. During these nine years the majority of the court had been quite as willing to sustain Congressional legislation as had Justice Holmes; but the Child Labor case presented a question upon which unanimity was utterly impossible. The five Justices who declared the law of Congress unconstitutional tacitly refused to extend further the police power of Congress under the Commerce Clause; the four dissenting justices, led by Justice Holmes, attempted to uphold the law upon precedent, though the fundamental justification for it could be only the general welfare. Without doubt, the Child Labor Law was inherently different from the regulations of commerce which had gone before, and the real question before the court was one of social expediency rather than of strict constitutional law. By precedent, the majority was correct. A limit might well have been deemed necessary for the ever-widening scope of Congressional legislation, and in this case an easy distinction could be made.

However, the stand taken by Justice Holmes is so entirely consistent with his earlier opinions and public utterances, a student of his works cannot but be gratified that he has thus rounded out a full record of consistent social opinion.

The Federal Child Labor Law of 1916 provided in substance that no one should ship in interstate commerce the product of any mine or quarry in the United States in which within 30 days before children under 16 have been permitted to work, or the product of any factory where children under 14 have been employed, or where children between 14 and 16 have worked more than 8 hours in a day or more than six days a week, or after 7 p. m. or before 6 a. m.—within 30 days preceding such shipment.

---

[14] Clark Distilling Co. vs. Western Md. Ry. Co., 242 U. S., 311.
[15] United States vs. Hill, 248 U. S., 420.

Plainly, the evil to be remedied by this statute preceded the shipment, and had ceased before the shipment took place. In the Pure Food Act, the White Slave Act, and the Lottery Act, the evil would take place only after the completion of the shipment. In both cases, the object was to guard the health, safety or morals of the community. The accomplishment of the subsequent evil depended upon the shipment of the goods; hence the connection with interstate commerce was reasonably close.

In the case of the Child Labor Law, however, the evil did not depend upon interstate commerce for its accomplishment. The goods shipped were intrinsically harmless. Therefore, in fact, by this law Congress had attempted to regulate the conditions of manufacturing of goods intended for interstate shipment. The attempt involved two novel principles, namely: the broadening of the Federal police power to cover evils occurring before as well as after interstate commerce; and the prohibition of the shipment of articles intrinsically harmless to the health and morals of the recipients.

The majority opinion, delivered by Justice Day, differentiates the Lottery, Pure Food, and White Slave cases from the present question, holding the Child Labor Law unconstitutional because "it not only transcends the authority delegated to Congress over commerce, but also exerts a power as to a purely local matter to which the Federal authority does not extend."

The court finds the evil ended before the goods are offered for shipment, and therefore cannot perceive a connection with interstate commerce close enough to justify Congressional legislation. Furthermore, the court seems to state that the prohibition of the shipment of certain kinds of goods must be confined to goods intrinsically harmful or of such a peculiar nature that govermental authority over them is admittedly greater than over other kinds of commodities. This classification seems to fit pretty well the existing precedents, but does not allow room for expansion of the police power. Liquor and immoral women are commodities over which all governments are recognized to have a certain special police jurisdiction; but to limit that jurisdiction concretely seems to be rather hazardous in the changing law of today.

In stating the main argument of the court, Justice Day, after distinguishing the precedents, said:

> In each of these instances the use of interstate transportation was necessary to the accomplishment of harmful results. In other words, although the power over interstate transportation was to regulate, that could only be accomplished by prohibiting the use of the facilities of interstate commerce to effect the evil intended.
>
> This element is wanting in the present case. . . . The act in its effect does not regulate transportation among the states, but aims to standardize the ages at which children may be employed in mining and manufacturing within the states. The goods shipped are of themselves harmless. . . . When offered for shipment, and before transportation begins, the labor of their production is over, and the mere fact that they were intended for interstate commerce transportation does not make their production subject to Federal control under the commerce power.

Moreover, Justice Day, in distinguishing the subject matter of the Child Labor Law from that properly belonging under the Commerce Clause, emphasizes the principle that the natural and reasonable effect of laws must be ascertained; and that the Child Labor Law is a regulation of manufacture and production, and not of commerce, though the statute calls itself a regulation of interstate commerce. This point is not essential to the conclusion reached by the majority, but it is the object of Justice Holmes' most effective criticism.

Justice Holmes' opinion is rather a criticism of the arguments of the majority than a statement of the grounds upon which he would justify the law. His affirmed belief in the finality of legislative determinations in matters over which the police power may extend is the undercurrent of his opinion, as the following statement bears witness: "It does not matter whether the supposed evil precedes or follows the transportation. It is enough that, in the opinion of Congress, the transportation encourages the evil."

Thus he disposes of the distinction which the majority draws between precedent and subsequent evils. This flat statement hardly settles the question to the satisfaction of anyone, and it is hard to believe that Justice Holmes has meant it to be his final argument for the extension of the

Federal police power to the regulation of conditions precedent to the offering of goods for interstate shipment. Indeed, though his general criticisms of the arguments of Justice Day are calculated to bring to light flaws and illogical conclusions, he has not gone far in the direction of justifying the Child Labor Law on any other grounds than that it ought to be, and that the authority exercised by Congress in it is one which the prevailing public morality demands, and is therefore legally justified.

First, Justice Holmes admits that the States have exclusive control over their methods of production, but argues that the fact that a Federal law indirectly affects that control is not a ground for holding the law void. In its immediate effects, surely, the Child Labor Law is valid, for Congress is given the power to regulate commerce in unqualified terms, and the statute merely prohibits the carrying of certain kinds of goods in interstate and foreign commerce. The power to prohibit has long been recognized as identical in these matters with the power to regulate. Therefore, if the act is to be held invalid, it must be upon some collateral grounds. Shall it be, he asks, "because of its possible reaction upon the conduct of the states in a matter upon which I have admitted that they are free from direct control? . . . I should have thought that the most conspicuous decisions of this court had made it clear that the power to regulate commerce and other constitutional powers could not be cut down or qualified by the fact that it might interfere with the carrying out of the domestic policy of any state."

Inquiry into the ultimate purpose of laws had been denied by the court in the Oleomargarine case [16] and the State Bank case.[17] In the latter the result, and the purpose, of the law was entirely outside the power of Congress. Furthermore, the Sherman Act had been used to break up combinations, with the commerce clause as the excuse, but not the purpose.

This criticism strikes the weakest spot in the majority

---

[16] McCray vs. U. S., 195 U. S., 27.
[17] Veazie Bank vs. Fenno, 8 Wall., 533.

opinion, but not the essential spot. To the outsider, the ease with which the Supreme Court is able to shift from one position to another in the matter of inquiring into the ultimate purpose of a law is nothing short of amazing. One decision invokes the "settled principle" that the court will look through form to substance, through words to the meaning hidden beneath them, through the avowed purpose of a law to its real purpose; and the next decision may speak of that other settled principle which forbids the court to look beyond the law itself.

Justice Holmes further makes the interesting point that the White Slave Law amounted in every way to a police regulation. It is rare to find a Justice of the Supreme Court upholding by its proper name a power which has been assumed by the legislature under cloak of the authority of a distinctly separate power. But it seems to be a characteristic of the Justice to call a spade a spade whenever possible.

Having destroyed, to his own satisfaction, the collateral arguments against the law advanced by the majority, and having established a police power in Congress specifically under the Commerce Clause, he goes on: "But I had thought that the propriety of the exercise of a power admitted to exist in some cases was for consideration of Congress alone, and that this court always had disavowed the right to intrude its judgment upon questions of policy or morals. It is not for this court to pronounce when prohibition is necessary to regulation if it ever may be necessary,—to say that it is permissible as against strong drink, but not as against the product of ruined lives."

In conclusion, he reiterates his deference to legislative judgment in matters of public policy. In this lies his real reason for upholding the Child Labor Law, the same reason which had prompted him years before in the Lochner, Adair and Coppage cases: "The public policy of the United States is shaped with a view to the benefit of the nation as a whole. If, as has been the case within the memory of men still living, a state should take a different view of the propriety of sustaining a lottery from that which generally prevails,

I cannot believe that the fact would require a different decision from that reached in Champion vs. Ames. . . . The
national welfare as understood by Congress may require a
different attitude within its sphere from that of some self-
seeking state."

This is the climax of the series of " social" opinions which
Justice Holmes has rendered on the highest courts of Massachusetts and the United States.   In these opinions he has
regarded what he believes to be the primary purpose of the
law, rather than the strict precedent and the consecrated
phrase.  He has attempted to revolutionize the interpretation
of the Constitution rather than the Constitution itself.   In
some directions his efforts have been crowned with a practical
success; but, universally, he has made his impress upon the
legal thought of the United States as has, perhaps, no other
judge of modern times.   The truths which he has enunciated
so frankly from the bench have formed a body of principles
which must inevitably govern the law of the future—whether
they come to authority by the gradual change in the interpretation of the existing law, or by amendment to the Constitution.

# CHAPTER IV

## The Conflict of State and Federal Powers over Commerce

The location of the border line between the domain of the state and of the national government, in the regulation of commerce, has been a never ending task of the Supreme Court. The unfortunate fact that it cannot be ascertained trigonometrically and marked out permanently has led to some uncertainty as to its position, and a good deal of judicial doubt about the considerations which should move the courts in deciding on which side a given case should be placed.

One of the most common pitfalls and one easy for anyone to stumble into, is that of granting to the States a collateral power to regulate interstate commerce where the national government has not acted. This, carried out to any logical conclusion, involves a court in numerous difficulties. The undoubted fact that the States do possess and exercise a certain limited power over commerce between the States causes the confusion referred to; but if it is kept in mind that this power is not at all similar to that of the national government, the greatest difficulties are to be avoided. Justice Holmes has never been forced into an admission of collateral power in the States—and possibly for this reason his opinions are thoroughly logical in the delicate matter of differentiating between state and Federal powers.

Briefly, he refuses to allow the states any direct regulation of interstate commerce, as such; and with regard to state laws which affect commerce to a greater or less extent, he recognizes that the question is one of degree, and is not possible of decision by any other than common sense and practical criteria. He says: " In modern business every part is related so organically to every other that what affects any portion must be felt more or less by all the rest. Therefore, unless everything is to be forbidden and legislation is to come to a stop, it is not enough to show that, in the working of a statute, there is some tendency, logically discernible, to interfere with commerce or existing contracts.  Practical lines must be drawn, and distinctions of degree must be made." [1]

Justice Holmes cannot be considered as differing greatly from the rest of the Supreme Court in his desire to maintain as paramount the authority of the Federal government to regulate commerce among the States.  His insistence that the power of Congress affirmatively to regulate commerce is exclusive does not bring him to different conclusions from the court, but is simply an evidence of possibly a more accurate method of thought than has been shown at times by some of the other members of the Supreme Court.

The maintenance of the Federal power as supreme in this field is one of the few constitutional matters which he has mentioned in extra-judicial utterances.  The importance with which he regards it may be realized from what he said in a speech in 1913: "I do not think the United States would come to an end if we lost our power to declare an Act of Congress void.  I do think the Union would be emperiled if we could not make that declaration as to the laws of the several states.  For one in my place sees how often a local policy prevails with those who are not trained to national views and how often action is taken that embodies what the Commerce Clause was meant to end." [2]

Notwithstanding this strong feeling against attempts on the part of the States to encroach upon the domain of the Federal government, Justice Holmes has not allowed his jealousy for the powers of Congress to influence him to find regulations of interstate commerce in all state regulations which affect it incidentally.  Between his desire to ensure full power to Congress, and his regard for the full police powers of the States, he has drawn the line at a point slightly more favorable to the States than has the court.

The most important point of difference between his views and those of the court was raised in the cases under a Kansas law which required foreign corporations seeking to do a local

---

[1] Diamond Glue Company vs. United States Glue Co., 187 U. S., 611.

[2] Law and the Court, 1913, Speeches, p. 98.

business to pay certain fees, and to pay as a privilege tax
a certain percentage of their total authorized capital, wherever
located. In the cases, the law was applied to interstate carriers, which the state attempted to tax for their intrastate
business.

The question of contract being excluded, Justice Holmes
maintained in these cases that the state, having the power
to exclude foreign corporations from doing local business, has
the right to tax such business at will. The fact of the interstate business did not present to him a reason for restraining
this undoubted right of the State.

Dissenting in Western Union Telegraph Co. vs. Kansas,[3]
he said: "Even in the law the whole generally includes its
parts. If the state may prohibit, it may prohibit with the
privilege of avoiding that prohibition in a certain way."

The majority opinion had arrived at the conclusion that
"the natural and reasonable effect of the statute" (the Kansas tax law) was to burden the interstate business of the company, and that the tax, "by its necessary operation" would
accomplish the same result as if a condition of doing local
business were made "that the telegraph company should sub-
mit to taxation upon both its interstate and intrastate business
and upon its interests and property everywhere, as represented
by its capital stock." The opinion further stated that the
power of a State to regulate the privilege of a foreign corporation to do a local business extends only as long as the regulation is not unconstitutional—and that this regulation is repugnant to the Commerce Clause.

While this decision denounced an indefensible attempt to
plunder the Telegraph company, and thus was probably wise
on grounds of general policy; it nevertheless announced a
new principle governing the power of the States to regulate
their internal affairs, the justification for which was certainly
as ethereal as any which Justice Holmes had ever advanced
to uphold pieces of social legislation. Indeed, the reasoning
of the court diverged too widely from settled principles for

---

[3] 216 U. S., 1, J. Holmes dissenting, 52.

even so liberal a thinker as he has shown himself to be, and in this matter public policy had less weight with him than the existing law.

In the first place, says his dissent, Kansas did not attempt to tax the Western Union. She had simply announced that before it could do a purely local business it must pay a certain sum of money. After pointing out that the whole includes its parts, and that the right to prohibit includes the right to regulate, Justice Holmes says: " I quite agree that we must look through form to substance. The whole matter is left in the Western Union's hands. If the license fee is more than the local business will bear, it can stop that business and avoid the fee. . . . The state seeks only to oust the corporation from that part of its business that the corporation has no right to do unless the state gives leave."

The State's power to regulate this matter has no connection with the Constitution of the United States, says the Justice, but is arbitrary: " I confess my inability to understand how a condition can be unconstitutional when attached to a matter over which a State has absolutely arbitrary power."

Justice Holmes reiterated and emphasized this view in the almost identical case of Pullman Co. vs. Kansas.[4] The fact that a corporation could enter Kansas untaxed for interstate commerce did not, in his opinion, complicate the right of the state to prohibit or regulate its intrastate activities. " Such an exclusion is not a burden on the foreign commerce at all; it simply is the denial of a collateral benefit."

The much earlier case of Pullman Co. vs. Adams,[5] had been decided by a unanimous court, upon similar facts, using the arguments repudiated in the Kansas cases. That the Pullman Company was not compelled to carry passengers from one point to another within the State, but could discontinue that part of its business, was the ground upon which the court sustained the state tax on the privilege of carrying such passengers.

---

[4] 216 U. S., 56, J. Holmes dissenting, 75.
[5] 189 U. S., 419.

The Kansas cases plainly overruled this opinion, the court evidently believing that the extinction of the pernicious practice of sandbagging interstate carriers was more valuable than preserving inviolate the unlimited and arbitrary power of the States to control the entry of foreign corporations. The latter consideration apparently had the greater weight with Justice Holmes, who, moreover, had precedent upon his side. He would not curtail an established power because misused once. It may be noted, however, that he was not at all in sympathy with the practices of Kansas: "From other points of view, if I were at liberty to take them, I should agree that it [the Kansas law] deserved the reprobation it receives from the majority. But I have not heard, and have not been able to frame, a reason that I honestly can say seems to me to justify the judgment of the court in point of law." [6]

In addition to these cases, where Justice Holmes decided that there was, in his opinion, no regulation of interstate commerce, there have been others in which the possible burden upon commerce imposed by a state law, has been upheld by him as so remote as to be inconsequential, or as an inseparable and necessary incident of the exercise of an admittedly proper state power.

So, where an act made criminal by state law was committed in the course of interstate commerce, he refused to consider the punishment of it a regulation of commerce. The state law, he said speaking for the court, "is not even directed against interference with that business, but against acts of a certain kind that the state disapproves in whatever connection." [7]

The fact that a Congressional statute had authorized the use of post roads by telegraph wires did not prevent the city of Richmond from making reasonable regulations for the use of its streets. [8] If the fact of reasonableness could be established,

---

[6] Pullman Co. vs. Kansas. 216 U. S., 56.

[7] Standard Oil Co. vs. Tenn., 217 U. S., 413.

[8] Western Union vs. Richmond, 224 U. S., 160. Other cases in which state laws are upheld are Diamond Glue Co. vs. U. S. Glue Co., 187 U. S., 611; Hatch vs. Reardon, 204 U. S., 152.

he said, municipal police regulations were not violations of the Commerce Clause.

In Missouri Pacific Railway Co. vs. Larabee Flour Mills Company,[9] the opinion of the court upheld a state law regarding the transfer and return of freight cars by connecting carriers, on the ground that the State might regulate this matter until Congress or the Interstate Commerce Commission had acted upon it. The opinion thus admitted a concurrent power in the state to regulate a matter that was properly part of interstate commerce. Justice Holmes, concurring in the result reached, took occasion to make clear his dissatisfaction with the argument employed by the court. He upheld the law on the theory that the cars were not appropriated to interstate commerce, at the period when affected by the state law, and therefore were subject to state control.

Elsewhere he emphasized the singularity of the power to control interstate commerce: " But that subject matter (interstate commerce) is under the exclusive control of Congress and is not one that it has left to the states until there shall be further action on its part." [10]

By this review of some of the cases where he has decided in favor of the state's authority to pass laws of certain indirect effect upon interstate commerce, it is apparent that he has clearly stated in each case that there was no direct interference. Affirming a law, he repudiates the idea that it regulates commerce, other than in the remote sense that a law affecting any portion of business in general affects more or less all the rest.

A complete discussion of the cases in which he has spoken for the court in declaring unconstitutional state laws affecting interstate commerce would not be interesting in this study, since his views have been in consonance with those of the court, and are typical of the hundreds of decisions of a similar nature. It is sufficient to note that he has held invalid the following kinds of state regulations: Laws requiring peddlers, taking orders for goods to be shipped from another state, to

---

[9] 211 U. S., 612, J. Holmes concurring, 624.
[10] Kansas City S. R. Co. vs. Kaw. Valley Dist., 233 U. S., 75.

pay a license fee for doing business;[11] Laws measuring the tax on property or income of all interstate carrier within a state by any means which, in the opinion of the court, shows an aim at taxing the interstate business;[12] Law regulating the railroad rates where part of the line runs in another jurisdiction;[13] Order regulating the transmission of stock quotations from a telegraph office to brokers, where the contract between the New York Stock Exchange and the telegraph company provided for transmission to the brokers;[14] Order of a state board to an interstate carrier to remove certain railway bridges which were part of an interstate railway;[15] Law placing liability for damage in the interstate shipment of goods upon the last carrier, in opposition to the Carmack Amendment, which places it upon the first carrier;[16] Order of railroad commission that all trains be within 30 minutes of schedule time at their point of origin within the State, as applied to interstate trains.[17]

---

[11] Rearick vs. Penna., 203 U. S., 507; Dozier vs. Alabama, 218 U. S., 124.

[12] Fargo vs. Hart, 193 U. S., 490; Galveston, H. & S. R. Co. vs. Texas, 210 U. S., 217; Meyer vs. Wells, Fargo & Co., 223 U. S., 297.

[13] Hanley vs. Kansas City Street Ry. Co., 187 U. S., 617.

[14] Western Union vs. Foster, 247 U. S., 105.

[15] Kansas City Street Ry. Co., vs. Kaw. Valley Dist., 233 U. S., 75.

[16] Charleston & W. C. Ry. Co. vs. Varneville Furniture Co., 237 U. S., 597.

[17] M. K. & T. Ry. Co. vs. Texas, 245 U. S., 484.

# CHAPTER V

## The Fourteenth Amendment

Whatever may have been the doubts of the years immediately succeeding the Civil War as to the meaning of the 14th Amendment, they have been definitely quieted by the momentous decisions which have interpreted that Amendment, and restricted its possible application. In recent years, the general meaning of its provisions has not been seriously called into question; the cases arising under it have been questions of degree, and the Supreme Court of the United States has decided concrete rather than general principles since the beginning of the century. Though many important matters have arisen for adjudication, and many important decisions have been rendered under the authority of the 14th Amendment, there has been no change in the fundamental conception of its scope as expressed in the Slaughter-House and Civil Rights Cases.

In the series of cases interpreting the Amendment, it was made apparent that the general principles of the Constitution had not been changed by it, and that Congress was given no direct legislative powers over subject matter theretofore belonging to the states. Privileges and immunities of citizens of the United States were held to be nothing more, in the light of the Amendment, than they had been before its adoption. In short, the words which could have been interpreted to change the very essentials of the Constitution have been robbed of their revolutionary possibilities by the Supreme Court, and placed in the category of mere declarations of existing principles.

On the other hand, the 14th Amendment has given to the Federal Courts a wide latitude in reviewing state decisions, by the provisions " nor shall any state deprive any person of life, liberty, or property, without due process of law; nor deny to any person within its jurisdiction the equal protection of the laws."

It is safe to say that the great majority of cases taken on appeal from state to Federal courts are based upon this provision; most ingenious arguments have been used to show that state laws, of no matter what kind, contravene this guarantee. It has been the province of the Supreme Court to separate the chaff from the wheat, and to set up a definition of " due process of law" and " the equal protection of the laws " which will uphold the rights of the individual against discriminatory and oppressive state action, while leaving the States their acknowledged police power unimpaired.

Since, by its very nature, " due process of law " does not easily lend itself to definition, the work of the Supreme Court has not been that of referring each new case to a standard pattern, and ascertaining whether it conforms. The task has been more complex. The judicial yardstick has been common sense rather than precedent; the questions raised have been practical ones, and they have been decided on practical considerations. In the main, doctrinaire interpretations of the Amendment have been repudiated by the Court, fictions have been disregarded, and it has been required that the state actions complained of should actually work a deprivation of generally recognized rights. The comparatively few occasions upon which the Supreme Court has seemed to go to unwarranted lengths in declaring state legislation unconstitutional under the 14th Amendment have sometimes blinded public and legal opinion to the thousands of occasions upon which the court has refused to overthrow the action of a state legislature. The power of review given to the Feedral courts by the 14th Amendment has undoubtedly had a salutary effect upon the legislative activities of the States under the police power, but it has not deprived the States of any substantial part of their legitimate spheres of action.

Some errors of judgment must be expected from any group of men, and the nature of the litigation under the 14th Amendment is such that the personal opinion of the judge must play a greater or less part in the decisions. Questions of degree are not always decided upon law alone; and degree is the vital point in this class of cases. The state police power is in eternal conflict with the rights of individuals. A line must be drawn between the two conflicting forces. It is not surprising that, in drawing this line, the Supreme Court has sometimes placed it at a point distant from that chosen by public opinion.

The means by which such a line is drawn may be suggested by the following, written by Justice Holmes thirty years ago:

The growth of the law is very apt to take place in this way. Two widely different cases suggest a general distinction which is a clear one when stated broadly. But as new cases cluster around the opposite poles, and begin to approach each other, the distinctions become more difficult to trace; the determinations are made one way or the other on a very slight preponderance of feeling, rather than of articulate reason; and at last a mathematical line is arrived at by the contact of contrary decisions, which is so far arbitrary that it might equally well have been drawn a little farther to one side or to the other, but which must have been drawn somewhere in the neighborhood of where it falls.[1]

Substantive rights are guarded by the 14th Amendment; but the amount of their protection will depend ultimately upon the value which a court attaches to them as against the police power. If the legislature regulates a matter in which the court unconsciously feels that the rights of the person are more important than the rights of the State, the law will be called unconstitutional. The evil of allowing the judicial to supplant the legislative judgment as to expediency is recognized, however, and the rule laid down that the local law-making body is the judge of expediency and facts, and that the court will not intervene unless the deprivation of individual rights is flagrant, and openly impossible to justify. Like all rules, this is made to be broken. It is possibly the most important characteristic of Justice Holmes that he insists everywhere that this rule should be followed to the letter.

The adjective rights of the individual, while protected along with substantive rights by the 14th Amendment, have not been

---

[1] The Common Law, p. 127.

the subject of so much important litigation. The Bill of Rights is not forced upon the States by the 14th Amendment,[2] and therefore the procedure there required is not necessary in a state court, or by state law. The States may decide for themselves the formalities of their own law.[3]

As has been suggested before, Justice Holmes is found upon the side of those who would grant to the States the broadest kind of police powers,[4] and who would restrict the intervention of the Federal government to the most obvious cases of the denial of individual rights. His most important dissenting opinions defining the state police powers have been examined in the Lochner and Coppage cases; but in many opinions which he has delivered for the court his language has defined the police power, and has stated his conception of the function of the 14th Amendment in a unique manner. Therefore, the views which he has expressed, and especially the words in which he has expressed them, must be noted, even though they do not show him to be in dissent to the opinions of the majority.

The two points upon which Justice Holmes insists are that the legislative judgment as to expediency is final, and that cases under the 14th Amendment, and consequently involving

---

[2] Maxwell vs. Dow, 176 U. S., 581.

[3] See Justice Holmes' Opinions in Rawlins vs. Georgia, 201 U. S., 638. Also Chicago, R. I. & P. Ry. Co. vs. Cole, decided Dec. 8, 1919, when he says: " There is nothing, however, in the Constitution of the United States, or its Amendments, that requires a state to maintain the line with which we are familiar between the functions of the jury and those of the court."

[4] North Dakota ex Rel. Flaherty vs. Hanson, 215 U. S., 515. North Dakota, a " dry " state, required by statute the filing and publication of all United States liquor tax receipts in the State. The majority of the Supreme Court held that this statute placed a burden upon the Federal taxing power, and hence was unconstitutional, since it required a fee to be paid for the registration and publication. Justice Holmes, with Chief Justice Fuller and Justice McKenna, dissented without opinion. His dissent here would seem logically to be based upon a belief that the state law was a proper exercise of the police power. Argument to this effect was advanced by North Dakota counsel, who stated that the law was simply an aid to the state in spotting illicit sellers of liquor, and to be justified under the police power as tending to promote the morals of the people.

the police power, are questions of degree. Further, he has set
forth some classic negative definitions of the purposes of the
14th Amendment. He has declared against theoretical or
ideal meanings of it,[5] and has ever been an apostle of practical
common sense in the interpretation of the Constitution. Perhaps the sentence which best summarizes his impatience with
attempts to extend the 14th Amendment to a theoretical extreme appears in a recent case, when he said: "The 14th
Amendment is not a pedagogical requirement of the impracticable."[6]

Several times Justice Holmes has spoken for the court in
momentous cases involving definition of the adjective rights
guaranteed to persons under the 14th Amendment.

During a time of considerable industrial disorder in Colorado, the governor of the State had called out the militia to
assist the civil authorities, and had declared the country in
a state of insurrection. An agitator, arrested at this period,
and imprisoned for some time by the military authorities,
alleged that his arrest had taken place without probable cause,
that the civil courts were open, and that the failure to bring
him before them had deprived him of his liberty without
due process of law.

Justice Holmes, speaking for the Supreme Court, maintained that due process of law varied with the subject matter
and with the necessities of the situation; that the governor,

---

[5] For instance, as Chief Justice of the Supreme Judicial Court of
Massachusetts, he said, in Tyler vs. Judges, etc., 175 Mass., 71:
"The prohibitions [of the 14th Amendment] must be taken largely
with a regard to substance, rather than to form, or they are likely
to do more harm than good." Note also the following against the
too logical interpretation of the guarantees of the Constitution:
"Whenever a wrong judgment is entered against a defendant, his
property is taken when it should not have been; but whatever the
ground may be, if the mistake is not so gross as to be impossible
in a rational administration of justice, it is no more than the imper-
fection of man, not a denial of constitutional rights" (Chicago Life
Ins. Co. vs. Cherry, 244 U. S., 25). "Now and then an extraordi-
nary case may turn up, but constitutional law, like other mortal
contrivances, has to take some chances, and in the great majority
of instances, no doubt, justice will be done" (Blinn vs. Nelson, 222
U. S., 1).

[6] Dominion Hotel Company vs. Arizona, Dec. March 24, 1919.

having the power to kill rioters in such times, is permitted to use the milder course of imprisoning them instead. Precautionary arrests may be made, if made in good faith, and the governor is the final judge of their necessity. " When it comes to a decision by the head of the state upon a matter involving its life, the ordinary rights of individuals must yield to what he deems the necessities of the moment. Public danger warrants the substitution of executive process for judicial process." [7]

This decision is a rebuttal of arguments which would guarantee any one given procedure as due process of law. It is also a demonstration of the fact that no definite limits can be set to " due process of law; " that in this connection circumstances determine the validity or invalidity of state action, whether it be executive, judicial, or legislative. The " expert on the spot " whom Justice Holmes mentions in his opinion, is the judge of expediency, not the United States Supreme Court.

The circumstances under which a Federal court may take jurisdiction of a case under the 14th Amendment have often been in doubt. Here again Justice Holmes is impatient of quibbles and undue technicalities: " It is a necessary and well-settled rule that the exercise of jurisdiction by this court to protect constitutional rights cannot be declined when it is plain that the fair result of a decision is to deny the rights." [8]

So, in the widely advertised Frank case,[9] he filed a strong dissent to the determination by the Supreme Court that it could not take jurisdiction.

A petition for a writ of habeas corpus was filed with the Federal District Court, after Frank's appeal had been defeated in the highest court of Georgia. The petition alleged that there had been great disturbances in and around the court room in which the original trial had taken place, that there was some indecision on the part of the judge as to the

---

[7] Mayer vs. Peabody, 212 U. S., 78.

[8] Rogers vs. Alabama, 192 U. S., 226.

[9] Frank vs. Maugum, 237 U. S., 309, J. Holmes dissenting, 345.

possibility of maintaining order, and the virtual admission by him that a verdict of acquittal would cause a hostile mob demonstration. Further, that for this reason, the prisoner was not allowed to be present when the verdict was rendered. It was alleged that these circumstances constituted coercion of the jury, and a denial of due process of law.

The district court held that all the matters raised in the petition had been decided by the state courts of competent jurisdiction, and that the Federal courts had no jurisdiction in the case. The majority of the Supreme Court, called upon to decide this question of Federal jurisdiction held that the lower court had properly refused to take the case.

Justice Holmes, with Justice Hughes, dissented. He found that the petition alleged and set forth a state of facts which amounted on their face to coercion of the jury, and that the fact of the competent jurisdiction of the state courts was immaterial:

> Whatever disagreement there may be as to the scope of ' due process of law,' there can be no doubt that it embraces the fundamental conception of a fair trial, with opportunity to be heard. Mob law does not become due process of law by securing the assent of a terrorized jury. . . . In such a case the Federal Court has jurisdiction to issue the writ. . . .
> When such a case is presented, it cannot be said, in our view, that the state court decision makes the matter *res judicata.* . . . When the decision of the fact is so interwoven with the decision of the question of constitutional right that the one necessarily involves the other, the Federal Court must examine the facts. . . . Otherwise, the right will be a barren one. It is significant that the argument for the state does not go so far as to say that in no case would it be permissible, on application for habeas corpus, to override the findings of fact by the state courts. It would indeed be a most serious thing if this court were so to hold, for we could not but regard it as a removal of what is perhaps the most important guaranty of the Federal Constitution.

Justice Holmes, in this opinion, indicated a far more liberal view of the Federal power of review of alleged state deprivations of adjective rights than he had ever shown himself to hold as to a similar deprivation of substantive rights under the state police power.

This characteristic may be referred back to his fundamental conception of the law as a living thing, working justice to the people, and his abhorrence of the conception of the law which sees it only as a mass of rules and technical formulas to which every case must be referred mathematically. Believing that the justification of the law is the social advantage, he sees that advantage increased by an interpretation of the law to grant to the individual all possible protection in the procedure of courts of justice. The constitutional guarantees as applied in the criminal law he has everywhere interpreted to the advantage of the individual, as against the state. It is only when substantive rights of individuals are pitted against the powers of the state that he is inclined to favor the latter, in the exercise of its police powers.

His best known definition of the police power is, according to prevailing constitutional law, probably too broad. However, it sums up his conception of its scope, a conception consistently kept in mind by him in upholding social legislation: "It [the police power] may be put forth in aid of what is sanctioned by usage, or held by the prevailing morality or strong and preponderant opinion to be greatly and immediately necessary to the public welfare." [10]

As a matter of fact, the exercise of the police power has not been sanctioned in many cases which this definition would include—but in those cases Justice Holmes has dissented and has stood for his own beliefs. Therefore, it is safe to take the above definition as the one which Justice Holmes believes the ideal for the police power, and which he has methodically attempted to make a part of the constitutional law of the United States.

That Justice Holmes' view of the police power is open to very serious criticism has been demonstrated time and again by the majority of the Supreme Court. But that it represents an influential school of the legal thought of the day, is not to be disputed.

He stated in another case that state legislatures may think that an evil can be remedied only by prohibition of it, and that in such a case the courts are not at liberty to interfere

---

[10] Noble State Bank vs. Haskell, 219 U. S., 104.

unless "it is a clear, unmistakable infringement of rights secured by the fundamental law." [11]

In that case, California had prohibited the buying and selling of stocks on margin. The law was upheld under the police power. In his opinion, Justice Holmes said, speaking for the court:

> While the courts must exercise a judgment of their own, it by no means is true that every law is void which may seem to the judges who pass upon it excessive, unsuited to its ostensible end, or based upon conceptions of morality with which they disagree. . . . Otherwise a constitution, instead of embodying only relatively fundamental rules of right, as generally understood by all English-speaking communities, would become the partisan of a particular set of ethical or economical opinions, which by no means are held *semper ubique et ab omnibus.*

An enlightening suggestion of the antithesis between private rights and the police power of the state is found in the succeeding paragraph: "All rights tend to declare themselves absolute to their logical extreme. Yet all in fact are limited by the neighborhood of principles of policy which are other than those on which the particular right is founded, and which become strong enough to hold their own when a certain point is reached. The limits set to property by other public interests present themselves as a branch of what is called the police power of the state." [12]

And the fundamental point to be remembered in considering the constitutionality of police legislation under the 14th Amendment, in the opinion of Justice Holmes, is made in the following statement: "Great constitutional provisions must be administered with caution. Some play must be allowed for the joints of the machine, and it must be remembered that legislatures are ultimate guardians of the liberties and welfare of the people in quite as great a degree as the courts." [13]

In this same case he established as follows the standard by which alleged discriminatory legislation is to be measured:

[11] Otis & Gassman vs. Parker, 187 U. S., 606.
[12] Hudson County Water Company vs. McCarter, 209 U. S., 349.
[13] M. K. & T. Ry. Co. vs. May, 194 U. S., 267.

" When a state legislature has declared that, in its opinion, policy requires a certain measure, its action should not be disturbed by the courts under the 14th Amendment, unless they can see clearly that there is no fair reason for the law that would not require with equal force its extension to others whom it leaves untouched."

While the above quotations have been taken from opinions of the court, and were not expressed in dissent, they have not necessarily been the ideas of Justice Holmes' colleagues upon all occasions. It is a characteristic of the Justice that, even in writing the majority opinion, he impresses his individuality upon the words to such an extent that one feels that he is speaking for himself alone. No doubt many of his general expressions do not agree wholly with the views of the justices whom he is representing, and it is safe often to take them as the individual pronouncements of Justice Holmes, and of no one else—imagining that the court is permitting him to represent it with a gifted pen, which must be allowed a certain poetic license.

To paraphrase the statements of Justice Holmes on the relation between the police power and the 14th Amendment is to lose their true significance and flavor. To appreciate the emphasis with which he argues against doctrinaire interpretations, one must read his own words:

We must be cautious about pressing the broad words of the 14th Amendment to a drily logical extreme. Many laws which it would be vain to ask the court to overthrow would be shown, easily enough, to transgress a scholastic interpretation of one or another of the great guaranties of the Bill of Rights. They more or less limit the liberty of the individual, or they diminish property to a certain extent. We have few scientifically certain criteria of legislation, and as it often is difficult to mark the line where what is called the police power of the states is limited by the Constitution of the United States, judges should be slow to read into the latter a *nolumus mutare* as against the lawmaking power.[14]

It is important for this court to avoid extracting from the very general language of the 14th Amendment a system of delusive exactness in order to destroy methods of taxation which were well known when that Amendment was adopted, and which it is safe to say that no one then supposed would be disturbed.[15]

---

[14] Noble State Bank vs. Haskell, 219 U. S., 104. See also Assaria State Bank vs. Dalley, 228 U. S., 1.

[15] Louisville & Nash. Ry. Co. vs. Barber Asphalt Co., 197 U. S., 430.

By declaring himself against the pressing of the 14th Amendment " to a drily logical extreme," he avoids a whole multitude of judicial crimes which that provision of the Constitution would make possible.

Here, however, as in other branches of the law, Justice Holmes has not allowed himself to be the special pleader of any cause. While he upholds the state in the exercise of its broad police powers, he condemns it vigorously when it attempts to oppress and discriminate under the " convenient apologetics of the police power."

When Louisiana passed a law regulating sugar refineries, and made its provisions apply to a certain kind of refinery only,—a description filled by the American Sugar Refining Company alone,—Justice Holmes led the Supreme Court in condemning the State's action as unconstitutional. The law, says Justice Holmes " bristles with severities that touch the plaintiff alone." [16] South Dakota prepared a law which made it practically impossible for railroads to settle damage suits, and further provided that if such suits were not settled, double damages could be adjudged. This attempt to mulct the roads did not fall within the scope of the police power, and the Justice said : " No doubt the states have a large latitude in the policy that they will pursue and enforce, but the rudiments of fair play required by the 14th Amendment are wanting when a defendant is required to guess rightly what a jury will find." [17]

The most obvious taking of property by the state is, of course, the taking incident to the taxing power. Almost any tax can be denounced as a taking without due process of law—if due process is given a sufficiently extended meaning. It is natural, therefore, that the Supreme Court should have had many taxation cases before it in which infringement of the 14th Amendment has been alleged.

The court has consistently refused to give weight to specious

---

[16] McFarland vs. American Sug. Ref. Co., 241 U. S., 78.   See also International Harvester Co. vs. Kentucky, 234 U. S., 217.

[17] Chicago, Mil. & St. P. Ry. Co. vs. Polt, 232 U. S., 165.   See also Missouri Pac. Ry. Co. vs. Nebraska, 217 U. S., 195.

arguments, and has generally upheld the taxing laws of the
States against the Amendment. The States have been left free
to raise revenue by any reasonably legitimate tax. " Equal
protection of the laws " has been interpreted to mean far less
than its apparent literal meaning. Realizing that, by showing sympathy with far-fetched interpretations of the guarantees, it would bring every taxing case in the United States
before it, the court has been loath to extend its power in this
direction. As Justice Holmes pertinently remarks: " We do
not sit as a general appellate board of revision for all rates
and taxes in the United States. We stop with considering
whether it clearly appears that the Constitution of the United
States has been infringed. . . ." [18]

The same tests of common sense and reality must be applied to the taxing power as to the police power, says the
court, speaking by Justice Holmes: " It is a sufficient answer
to say that you cannot carry a constitution out with mathematical nicety to logical extremes. If you could, we never
should have heard of the police power, and this is still more
true of taxation, which, in most communities, is a long way
off from a logical and coherent theory." [19]

In general, Justice Holmes has emphasized the point that
the 14th Amendment did not change long standing practices
of the state which were embedded in the law.[20] Nor does he
believe that its provisions require any new procedure antecedent to the levying of taxes. Thus, he says, in answer to
the allegation that a property owner was deprived of due
process of law because he had no hearing before a general

[18] San Diego Land & T. Co. vs. Jasper, 189 U. S., 339.

[19] Paddell vs. New York, 211 U. S., 446.

[20] Instance the following statements: " It would be a surprising
extension of the 14th Amendment if it were held to prohibit the
continuance of one of the most universal and best known distinctions of the mediaeval law " (Grant Timber & Mfg. Co. vs. Gray,
236 U. S., 133). " We cannot wholly neglect the long settled law
and a common understanding of a particular state in considering
the plaintiff's rights. We are bound to be very cautious in coming
to the conclusion that the 14th Amendment has upset what thus
has been established and accepted for a long time " (Otis Company
vs. Ludlow Mfg. Co., 201 U. S., 140).

tax law went into effect: " Where a rule of conduct applies
to more than a few people, it is impracticable that everyone
should have a direct voice in its adoption.  The Constitution
does not require all public acts to be done in town meeting
or an assembly of the whole.  General statutes affect the
person or property of individuals, sometimes to the point of
ruin, without giving them a chance to be heard.  Their rights
are protected in the only way that they can be in a complex
society, by their power, immediate or remote, over those who
make the rule." [21]

That all local remedies should be exhausted by a plaintiff
before the Federal courts can have jurisdiction of a taxation
case, is the ground of Justice Holmes' dissent in Raymond
vs. Chicago Union Trans. Co.[22]  A state board of equalization,
acting on a writ of mandamus from the state supreme court,
had made an assessment, which was proved to be discriminatory.  The majority of the Supreme Court held that the act
of the board was the act of the state, and that, being a denial
of equal protection of the laws, it gave jurisdiction to the
Federal courts.

Justice Holmes held that the lower Federal court did not
have jurisdiction, and that the wronged party should have
taken the case to the highest court of the state before the
issues could be raised under the Constitution of the United
States.  He cannot believe that the actions, admittedly unconstitutional, of a subordinate board, can be held to be the final
action of the state, when the highest state tribunal has never
passed upon it.

He has had a prominent part in expounding the necessary
doctrine that a taking of property without compensation is
often the necessary collateral result of otherwise desirable
laws, under the taxing and the police powers.  This doctrine,
the inevitable result of the practice of all governments in
improving streets, and roads, regulating the building of improvements, etc., works an undeniable deprivation of property
to many owners.  Indeed, uniform taxes for street improve-

---

[21] Bi-Metallic Invest. Co. vs. State Board, 239 U. S., 441.
[22] 207 U. S., 20; J. Holmes dissenting, 40.

ments often are levied where some of the abutting property is of such a nature that the improvements are of no benefit, and actually cause a money loss to the owners. Several of Justice Holmes' statements on this point have frankly justified the practice on grounds of public policy, notably in the cases of Martin vs. District of Columbia [23] and Louisville & Nashville Ry. Co. vs. Barber Asphalt Company. [24]

State regulation of the rates of public service corporations has given rise to bitter litigation under the 14th Amendment and the obligations of contracts clause of the Constitution. Without an attempt to discuss the whole subject, it may be remarked that the Supreme Court has not been inclined to read implied contracts into state and municipal franchises to public service corporations. A definite bi-lateral contract must usually be shown the court before it will decide that the government has contracted away its right to regulate rates, or has in any way encumbered that right.

Naturally, when a confiscatory rate can be proved, the Supreme Court will give the company relief. Justice Holmes has expressed views distinct from those of the court only rarely in this matter, and usually to maintain some related idea upon which he is everywhere insistent. So, to uphold the belief that he expresses in every branch of the law, that the whole includes its part, he dissented in the case of Denver vs. Denver Union Water Company. [25] The water company's franchise had expired, but, pending renewal, the company was designated by municipal ordinance as " without a fran-

---

[23] 205 U. S., 135.

[24] 197 U. S., 430. Some of the other cases involving the taxing power of the States and the 14th Amendment, in which Justice Holmes has rendered the decision of the court, are: C. B. & Q. Ry. Co. vs. Babcock, 204 U. S., 585; New York, etc. vs. Miller, 202 U. S., 584; Blackstone vs. Miller, 188 U. S., 189; Wright vs. Louisville & N. Ry. Co., 195 U. S., 219; Gast Realty & I. Co. vs. Schneider Gran. Co.. 240 U. S., 55; Equitable Life Ass. Soc. vs. Penna., 238 U. S., 143; Board of Assessors vs. N. Y. Life Ins. Co., 216 U. S., 517; Hammond Packing Co. vs. Montana, 233 U. S., 331; Savannah, etc. Ry. Co. vs. Savannah, 198 U. S., 392; Coulter vs. L. & N. Ry. Co., 196 U. S., 599; Kidd vs. Alabama, 188 U. S., 730; Missouri vs. Dockery, 191 U. S., 165.

[25] 246 U. S., 178.

chise and a mere tenant by sufferance of the streets of the city." In this situation, the city fixed water rates, which the company alleged were confiscatory. The majority of the Supreme Court upheld this view, and declared the ordinance to be in violation of the 14th Amendment.

Justice Holmes' dissent is based upon the view that the company is not compelled by the ordinance to furnish water, that it may be ordered to stop furnishing water at any time, or may cease of its own accord. " The ordinance of the city would mean no more than that the company must accept the city's rates or stop; and as it could be stopped by the city out and out, the general principle is that it could be stopped unless a certain price should be paid."

The habit of many public service corporations, complaining whenever a new rate is instituted, does not make any impression upon Justice Holmes. He agrees with the court in requiring the companies to produce indubitable proof that the rates are confiscatory, and do not give a fair return. Alleged discriminations between similar public service corporations in a community must be shown to be based upon unreasonable premises. The mere fact of discrimination, and special legislation, is not necessarily enough to make the legislation unconstitutional under the 14th Amendment. The legislature which passes a discriminatory law judges the expediency of it,[26] and it is the work of the courts to determine, not whether the motive of the legislature was proper, but whether there could be any reasonable basis for the discrimination. If facts showing the lack of this reasonable basis are not produced, the court is compelled to accept the judgment of the law-making body. As Justice Holmes says: " A general law must be judged by public facts, but

---

[26] " But while there are differences of opinion as to the degree and kind of discrimination permitted by the 14th Amendment, it is established by repeated decisions that a statute aimed at what is deemed an evil, and hitting it presumably where experience shows it to be most felt, is not to be upset by thinking up and enumerating other instances to which it might have been applied equally well, so far as the court can see " (Keokee Consol. Coke Co. vs. Taylor, 234 U. S., 224).

judicially known. Therefore the law must be sustained on this point unless the facts offered in evidence clearly show that the exception cannot be upheld. But the local facts are not before us, and it follows that we cannot say that the legislature could not have been justified in thus limiting its action." [27]

The police power, carried out to a very broad scope, tends to set up an arbitrary power in the state to destroy property. It has been noticed that Justice Holmes has justified the incidental, and fractional taking of property, under the police and the taxing powers, as a necessary incident of government. In his words, " the great constitutional provisions for the protection of property . . . must be taken to permit the infliction of some fractional and relatively small losses without compensation, for some, at least, of the purposes of wholesome legislation." [28]

But finally the police power shades into the right of eminent domain. Certain things must be taken, or prohibited by sound public policy; but when the taking is not merely incidental, there must be compensation. So, in the case of a Massachusetts law which permitted the killing without compensation of horses with glanders, and under which the commissioners destroyed a horse which proved not to have glanders, Justice Holmes says, in answer to the question whether the statute covered such a killing: " We cannot admit that the Legislature has an unlimited right to destroy property without compensation, on the ground that destruction is not an appropriation to public use. . . . When a healthy horse is killed by a public officer acting under a general statute, for fear that it should spread disease, the horse certainly would seem to be taken for public use as truly as if it were seized to drag an artillery wagon. The

---

[27] Interstate Consol. Street Ry. Co. vs. Mass., 207 U. S., 79. For other cases on this general subject, see: Tampa Water Works Co. vs. Tampa, 199 U. S., 241; Northern Pac. Ry. Co. vs. N. D., 216 U. S., 579; Madera Waterworks vs. Madera, 228 U. S., 454.

[28] Interstate Consol. Street Ry. Co. vs. Mass., ibid.

public equally appropriates it whatever they do with it after-wards." [29]

Again in Massachusetts the Justice drew attention to the delicate shading between the cases where compensation is due and eminent domain is necessary, and those in which public policy alone will justify a taking: " Some small limitations of previously existing rights incident to property may be imposed for the sake of preventing a manifest evil; larger ones could not be except by the exercise of the right of eminent domain." [30]

Justice Holmes has held that the power of eminent domain possessed by the state can be exercised for a variety of ends. He has not argued for a strict interpretation of the term " public use," holding, generally, that the ideas of the state legislature as to its meaning should be accepted by the courts. " In the opinion of the legislature and the supreme court of Utah the public welfare of that state demands that aerial lines between the mines upon its mountain sides and the railways in the valleys below should not be made impossible by the refusal of a private owner to sell the right to cross his land. The Constitution of the United States does not require us to say that they are wrong." [31]

The essentially local character of this power is emphasized in a dissenting opinion: " The fundamental fact is that eminent domain is a prerogative of the state, which, on the one hand, may be exercised in any way that the state thinks fit, and, on the other may not be exercised except by an authority which the state confers." [32]

---

[29] Miller vs. Horton, 152 Mass., 540.
[30] Rideout vs. Knox, 148 Mass., 368 (1889).
[31] Strickley vs. Highland Boy Gold Mining Company, 200 U. S., 527.
[32] Madisonville Traction Co. vs. St. Bernard Mining Co., 196 U. S., 239, J. Holmes dissenting.

# CHAPTER VI

## Rights Guaranteed by the First Eight Amendments

The personal rights guaranteed by the first eight Amendments to the Constitution have generally been given a strict interpretation by the courts. The Supreme Court has taken the view that the Amendments were made for a definite purpose, which can be ascertained historically; and that giving effect to this purpose is the duty of the courts. In the cases of the 1st Amendment and the due process clause of the 5th Amendment, there has been some uncertainty and wavering on the part of the Supreme Court in defining a meaning, but, in regard to the other Amendments, a policy of strict enforcement has been followed.

The expediency of transferring some of the duties of the courts to the shoulders of administrative officers became apparent when the immigration problem began to assume large proportions. In particular, the multitudinous cases arising under the Chinese exclusion acts, would have placed too heavy a burden upon the Federal Courts if all of them had been heard. Therefore, administrative officers charged with the control of immigration were given jurisdiction of inquiries as to facts, and the power of admission and exclusion of aliens. The finality of administrative determinations in this field, when the hearings had been in conformity with common sense rules of fair play, was upheld.

Justice Holmes has delivered some important decisions, to be considered later, upholding the action of administrative officers. In this particular he has abandoned an otherwise thoroughly consistent stand for the strict interpretation of the guarantees of the Bill of Rights. The obvious practical necessity for this extension of administrative power needs no defense, or explanation, other than that given in the opinions to be noted subsequently.

The most important opinions of Justice Holmes, falling within the Bill of Rights, are those interpreting that part of the 1st Amendment which guarantees freedom of speech and of the press.

Freedom of speech has been, to him, a phrase having a practical meaning. He has maintained the attitude that the question involved in considering alleged restriction upon that freedom is one degree, and not to be decided upon fictitious or scholastic hypotheses. He has neither embraced the school of interpretation which would have the 1st Amendment prevent only previous restraints upon speech, although he was apparently inclined to adopt that view in theory at one time in his carreer; nor has he held the equally untenable position that the Amendment gives absolute immunity from the consequences of words, no matter what their character. His position has been on a middle ground, his distinction between valid and invalid restrictions upon speech being one of degree, based upon his personal conception of the location of the line where individual liberty and public policy clash.

In all cases in which he has spoken on this Amendment he has been careful to limit liability for an expression of opinion to instances where the speech or publication charged was, or was intended to be, an incitement to a breach of the law, or an undeniable contempt of court. He has been unwilling to allow judicial or legislative action to pass even slightly beyond the limits of undisputed necessity; and where he has detected an interference with, or a liability arising from, speech which is not necessarily wrongful, and not necessarily intended to incite to crime, he has upheld individual rights in emphatic language. " With effervescing opinions, as with the not yet forgotten champagnes, the quickest way to let them get flat is to let them get exposed to the air," he wrote to the Harvard Liberal Club on January 12, 1920.[1]

In Fox vs. Washington,[2] there was a unanimous decision, upholding a state law punishing publications advocating the commission of any crime, or encouraging or advocating disrespect for law or for any court of justice. The jury had found in the lower court that the publication encouraged and

[1] New Republic, January 28, 1920, p. 250.
[2] 236 U. S., 273.

indirectly incited a breach of the laws against indecent exposure. Justice Holmes does not consider the interesting question of the possibility of raising the 1st Amendment against a state law, but apparently accepts it as properly before the court. As to the provisions of the law which pretend to punish publications advocating disrespect for the law and for the courts, he says: " It does not appear and is not likely that the statute will be construed to prevent publications merely because they tend to produce unfavorable opinions of a particular statute or of law in general."

Here there is presented a clear case,—an overt act contrary to the law, and a publication advising the commission of that act. Though the principal point in the case is too clear to remark upon, the insistence with which Justice Holmes limits himself in this opinion is interesting, as is his intimation that the court could not uphold the other provisions of the statute.

In three cases [3] arising under the Espionage Act of 1917, decided in March 1919, Justice Holmes, who delivered the court's opinion, was cautious in his language and careful to assert that a state of war permitted far more extensive restrictions upon the freedom of speech than could be properly imposed in times of peace. Indeed, his opinions upholding the convictions under this act are based on the war power. Briefly, he shows that during war Congress has the power to punish actual obstructions to recruiting and similar hindrances to the prosecution of the war. Hence, words actually hindering recruiting are criminal—an indisputable proposition of law. Further, since the Espionage Act punishes conspiracies to obstruct as well as the actual obstruction, and as the tendency and the intent are the same as if the result is actually accomplished " we perceive no ground for saying that success alone warrants making the act a crime." [4]

By this reasoning he upheld, in the Schenck case, punish-

---

[3] Schenck vs. U. S., 249 U. S., 575; Frohwerk vs. U. S., 249 U. S., 204; Debs vs. U. S., 249 U. S., 211,—all decided March 3, 1919.
[4] Schenck vs. U. S., ibid.

ment for publishing and distributing certain pamphlets whose intent was found to be the obstruction of recruiting.

The Frohwerk case concerned the publication of the usual anti-army, pro-German propaganda in the Missouri *Staats Zeitung*. Conviction was affirmed, though the facts disclosed no special effort to reach men subject to the draft. "But we must take the case on the record as it is, and on that record it is impossible to say that it might not have been found that the circulation of the paper was in quarters where a little breath would be enough to kindle a flame, and that the fact was known and relied upon by those who sent the paper out."[5]

In each of these cases, as remarked above, Justice Holmes set up the circumstance of war rather than any inherent right of Congress to abridge the freedom of speech under other circumstances, except those in which it would be criminal by analogy with the common law: "I do not doubt for a moment that by the same reasoning that would justify punishing persuasion to murder, the United States constitutionally may punish speech that produces or is intended to produce a clear and imminent danger that it will bring about forthwith certain substantive evils that the United States constitutionally may seek to prevent. The power undoubtedly is greater in time of war than in time of peace because war opens dangers that do not exist at other times."[6]

In these majority opinions the Justice might perhaps be called over-cautious in qualifying his affirmation of the decisions in the lower court: "We admit that in many places and in ordinary times the defendants, in saying all that was said in the circular, would have been within their constitutional rights" (Schenck case); "It may be that all this might be said or written even in time of war in circumstances that would not make it a crime. We do not lose our right to condemn either measures or men because the country is at war" (Frohwerk case).

---

[5] Frohwerk vs. U. S., 249 U. S., 204.
[6] Abrams vs. U. S., 250 U. S., 616; J. Holmes dissenting, 624.

Justice Holmes required, then, these elements to be present for the valid enforcement of the Espionage Act in the case of publications, that is: conspiracy, intent, and a contemplated overt act or result over which Congress had the power of criminal legislation, and thus gained power over the accessories before the fact, actual or constructive. It was not the words, but their reasonable result which made the publications criminal and destroyed their privilege under the 1st Amendment.

In each of these cases, the evidence appearing on the record was examined carefully, and the conclusion was reached, as expressed in the Schenck case, that " we find ourselves unable to say that the articles could not furnish a basis for a conviction upon the first count at least."

Justice Holmes found a difference between the questions presented to the court in the foregoing cases and the one raised in Abrams vs. United States.[7] Theretofore, it was the result that had been held criminal; in the Abrams case he felt that the uttering of the words themselves, and not any probable or reasonable result, constituted the crime. Therefore he dissented from the decision of the court in an opinion that was widely commented upon by the press of the country.

The facts concerned the publication of two pamphlets, by unnaturalized Russians. The first was an abusive attack upon the United States Government, protesting against the sending of American troops to Russia. It used highly objectionable language concerning the President and the " capitalistic government." The second called attention to the fact that Russian workmen in American munition factories were making ammunition to kill their own relations in Russia, and called upon them to strike in protest against the Government's making war on the Russian revolution.

The authors of these exhortations were indicted under the Espionage Act under four counts: (1) printing, etc., " Disloyal abusive etc. language about the form of the government of the United States " ; (2) " language intended to bring

---

[7] 250 U. S., 616, J. Holmes dissenting, 624.

the Government of the United States into scorn, contumely and disrepute" ; (3) "language intended to incite, provoke and encourage resistance to the United States in the war" ; (4) conspiring "to incite . . . curtailment of . . . ordnance and ammunition."

In both the majority opinion, delivered by Justice Clarke, and in Justice Holmes' dissenting opinion, in which Justice Brandeis concurred, the first two counts of the indictment were not considered seriously. The sentence imposed by the lower court was the maximum permitted for any one count, and the majority opinion in terms upholds only the third and fourth counts, leaving the constitutionality of conviction under the other counts undecided. Justice Clarke limits the question before the court to a determination of whether there was any evidence on which the jury's finding of guilty under the third and fourth counts could be sustained. He finds that there was not only some, but much such evidence.

Justice Holmes dismisses the first and second counts as unworthy of argument, and proceeds to a discussion of the fourth. The statute under which the plaintiffs in error were indicted requires an intent to hinder the prosecution of the war to be shown in prosecutions for inciting strikes. This intent, Justice Holmes says, has not been proved. In criminal statutes, words must be used exactly. "But, when words are used exactly, a deed is not done with intent to produce a consequence unless that consequence is the aim of the deed. It may be obvious, and obvious to the actor, that the consequences will follow, and he may be liable for it even if he regrets it, but he does not do the act with the intent to produce it unless the aim to produce it is the proximate motive of the specific act, although there may be some deeper motive behind."

If the words of the statute were not used exactly, they would be absurd.[8] "It is only the present danger of im-

---

[8] "It seems to me that this statute must be taken to use its words in strict and accurate sense. They would be absurd in any other. A patriot might think that we were wasting money on aeroplanes, or making more cannon of a certain kind than we needed, and might

mediate evil or intent to bring it about that warrants Congress in settling a limit to the expression of opinion where private rights are not concerned." The publication of a "silly leaflet by an unknown man" does not seem to Justice Holmes to constitute such a present danger. If, however, it was published for the single purpose of obstruction, it might be punishable. That purpose hardly seems to be present. "To say that two phrases, taken literally, might import a suggestion of conduct that would have interference with the war as an indirect and probably undesired effect, seems to me by no means enough to show an attempt to produce that effect."

The intent of the pamphlets was to prevent interference in the Russian revolution by the United States.

The third count, charging provocation of resistance to the United States in the war with Germany, must be regarded in the light of the section of the Espionage Act under which the indictment is drawn. This section, in Justice Holmes' view, by its context punishes "some forcible act of opposition." There is no hint of resistance in this sense in the pamphlets.

In this case sentences of twenty years imprisonment have been imposed for the publishing of two leaflets that I believe the defendants had as much right to publish as the government has to publish the Constitution of the United States now vainly invoked by them. Even if I am technically wrong, and enough can be squeezed from these poor and puny anonymities to turn the color of legal litmus paper, I will add, even if what I think the necessary intent were shown,—the most nominal punishment seems to me all that possibly could be inflicted, unless the defendants are to be made to suffer not for what the indictment alleges, but for the creed that they avow,— a creed that I believe to be the creed of ignorance and immaturity when honestly held, as I see no reason to doubt that it was held here, but which, although made the subject of examination at the

---

advocate curtailment with success; yet, even if it turned out that the curtailment hindered and was thought by other minds to have been obviously likely to hinder the United States in the prosecution of the war, no one would hold such conduct a crime. I admit that my illustration does not answer all that might be said, but it is enough to show what I think and to let me pass to a more important aspect of the case. I refer to the 1st Amendment to the Constitution that Congress shall make no law abridging the freedom of speech."

trial, no one has a right even to consider in dealing with the charges before the court.

Prosecution for the expression of opinions seems to me perfectly logical. If you have no doubt of your premises or your power and want a certain result with all your heart you naturally express your wishes in law and sweep away all opposition. To allow opposition by speech seems to indicate that you think the speech impotent, as when a man says that he has squared the circle, or that you do not care whole-heartedly for the result, or that you doubt either your power or your premises. But when men have realized that time has upset many fighting faiths, they may come to believe more than they believe the very foundations of their own conduct that the ultimate good desired is better reached by free trade in ideas— that the best test of truth is the power of the thought to get itself accepted in the competition of the market; and that truth is the only ground upon which their wishes safely can be carried out. That, at any rate, is the theory of our Constitution. It is an experiment, as all life is an experiment. Every year, if not every day, we have to wager our salvation upon some prophecy based upon imperfect knowledge. While that experiment is part of our system I think that we should be eternally vigilant against attempts to check the expression of opinions that we loathe and believe to be fraught with death, unless they so imminently threaten immediate interference with the lawful and pressing purposes of the law that an immediate check is required to save the country. I wholly disagree with the argument of the government that the 1st Amendment left the common law as to seditious libel in force. History seems to me against the notion. I had conceived that the United States through many years had shown its repentance for the Sedition Act of July 14, 1798, . . . by repaying fines that it imposed. Only the emergency that makes it immediately dangerous to leave the correction of evil councils to time warrants making any exception to the sweeping command, "Congress shall make no law abridging the freedom of speech." Of course I am speaking only of expressions of opinion and exhortations, which were all that were uttered here; but I regret that I cannot put into more impressive words my belief that in their conviction upon this indictment, the defendants were deprived of their rights under the Constitution of the United States.

The test which Justice Holmes has evolved, and by which he would judge the constitutionality of an attempt to make speech criminal, that is, whether it " produces or is intended to produce a clear and imminent danger that it will bring about forthwith certain substantive evils that the United States constitutionally may seek to prevent," is, in the final analysis, another way of saying that such questions are questions of fact, and depend for their decision upon the findings of the judge. By this statement he has enunciated no new theoretical principle to guide the court in establishing the constitutionality of future legislation.

The position taken by a judge on such questions, measured by Justice Holmes' test, discloses his individual political philosophy. The judge who is ready to find any speech advocating change criminal under the Espionage Act shows himself to be a reactionary. The judge at the opposite end of the scale would be a radical. Justice Holmes' record on the Espionage Act cases does not classify him as an extremist. His steadfast liberality of mind prevents him from seeing phantoms, and from allowing free speech to be abridged in any but the most obvious cases. That he could not see a " present and immediate danger " in the utterances in the Abrams case does not convict him of radicalism in any form. It is difficult to escape from the conviction that he foresaw an undue extension of the doctrine of the Schenck case, and believed that a warning should be sounded before that extension had gone too far. Public policy and fundamental justice moved him here rather than strict law.[9]

That the 1st Amendment cannot be pleaded as a defense for words which constitute contempt of court, is a general proposition to which Justice Holmes adheres. However, an attempt to punish a newspaper by summary contempt proceedings, long after the occurrence of the alleged contempt, caused him to protest in eloquent language.[10]

In Patterson vs. Colorado,[11] a newspaper claimed the right under the 1st Amendment to prove statements that had been adjudged contemptuous. This right was denied by Justice Holmes, who showed that the fact of the truth of a statement was no defense in the common law of criminal libel, and even less in contempt cases at common law. A true publication which reaches a jury, or a judge, during the trial of a case, and which would tend to influence them, is a contempt of court. Courts are liable to any sort of criticism

[9] See also the dissenting opinions of Justice Brandeis, in which Justice Holmes concurred, in Schaefer vs. U. S., decided March 1, 1920; and Pierce vs. U. S., decided March 8, 1920. These cases involve convictions under the Espionage Act. Justice Brandeis reiterates the argument of Justice Holmes in the Abrams case.

[10] Toledo Newspaper Co. vs. U. S., 247 U. S., 402, 422.

[11] 205 U. S., 454.

after the conclusion of a case, but not during the trial. Speaking of the 1st Amendment he says: " In the first place, the main purpose of such constitutional provisions is to prevent all such *previous restraints* upon publications as had been practised by other governments, and they do not prevent the subsequent punishment of such as may be deemed contrary to the public welfare." [12]

In Toledo Newspaper Co. vs. U. S.,[13] the judge of the lower court used his power to punish for contempt to prosecute a newspaper illegally, in Justice Holmes' opinion. The chief argument in his dissent here is based upon an Ohio statute, which limits the power of the court to punish summarily for contempt to " misbehavior of any person in their presence, or so near thereto as to obstruct the administration of justice." The publications punished had appeared in March, and it was not until September that the judge instituted summary proceedings and fined the newspaper heavily. The majority of the Supreme Court upheld the lower court. Justice Holmes says:

> When it is considered how contrary it is to our practice and ways of thinking for the same person to be accuser and sole judge in a matter which, if he be sensitive, may involve strong personal feeling, I should expect the power to be limited by the necessities of the case ' to insure order and decorum in their presence,' as it is stated in Ex Parte Robinson, 19 Wall., 505. . . . And when the words of the statute are read it seems to me that the limit is too plain to be construed away. . . . Misbehavior means something more than adverse comment or disrespect.

But even if there is an imminent possibility of obstruction, and this is sufficient, immediate action is contemplated, and summary proceedings cannot come so late as these. He continues:

> I find it impossible to believe that such a judge could have found in anything that was printed even a tendency to prevent his per-

---

[12] This statement was the subject of strong dissent from Justice Harlan, who saw in it a pernicious tendency to restrict freedom of speech. Justice Holmes' position was abandoned in Schenck vs. U. S. " It well may be that the prohibition of laws abridging the freedom of speech is not confined to previous restraints, although prevent them may have been the main purpose as intimated in Patterson vs. Colorado. . . ."

[13] 247 U. S., 402, dissenting opinion, 422.

forming his sworn duty. I am not considering whether there was a technical contempt at common law, but whether what was done falls within the words of an act intended and admitted to limit the power of the courts. . . . I would go as far as any man in favor of the sharpest and most summary enforcement of order in court and obedience to decrees, but when there is no need for immediate action contempts are like any other breach of law and should be dealt with as the law deals with other illegal acts. Action like the present, in my opinion, is wholly unwarranted by even color of law.

This latter idea is more fully brought out in Gompers vs. Buck Stove & Range Co.,[14] where, speaking for the court, he sets forth reasons why contempt of court is a crime, and as such protected by the statute of limitations: "It does not follow that contempts of the class under consideration are not crimes, or rather, in the language of the statute, offenses, because trial by jury as it has been gradually worked out and fought out has been thought not to extend to them as a matter of constitutional right. These contempts are infractions of the law, visited with punishment as such. If such acts are not criminal, we are in error as to the most fundamental characteristic of crimes as that word has been understood in English speech."

In short, the Justice has recognized the necessity of punishing contempts by summary proceedings; but he has not sanctioned the attempts to place contempt of court in a class to itself, and to make it an offense punishable at any time by the caprice of a single judge. His view is analogous to that of the criminal law, where a murderer, caught red-handed, may be apprehended dead or alive by an officer of the law; but once captured alive, he may not be executed without due trial.

In one of his latest opinions [15] Justice Holmes is found vigorously upholding the right of the individual and of the corporation to be protected from illegal search of premises and the seizure of incriminating or other property. In this case, the premises of the company were searched by government agents without a warrant, papers were seized, copied and photographed, and finally returned to the owner. On

---

[14] 221 U. S., 418.
[15] Silverthorne Lumber Co. vs. U. S., Dec. Jan. 26, 1920.

the information thus gained, charges were brought against the company, which was subpoenaed for the originals. The question here involved consideration of both the 4th and 5th Amendments, both the search and seizure, and the use in a criminal prosecution of evidence so obtained. Justice Holmes says, in his majority opinion, from which Chief Justice White and Mr. Justice Pitney dissented:

> The proposition could not be presented more nakedly. It is that though of course its seizure was an outrage which the government now regrets, it may study the papers before it returns them, copy them, and then may use the knowledge that it has gained to call upon the owners in a more regular form to produce them; that the protection of the Constitution covers the physical possession, but not any advantages that the government can gain over the object of its pursuit by doing the forbidden act. . . . It reduces the 4th Amendment to a form of words. . . . The essence of a provision forbidding the acquisition of evidence in a certain way is that not merely evidence so acquired shall not be used before the court, but that it shall not be used at all . . . the knowledge gained by the government's own wrong cannot be used by it in the way proposed.

Justice Holmes states further that the rights of an individual in this regard are no more that those of a corporation. This decision extends the exemption of corporations slightly beyond the dictum of Hale vs. Henkel,[16] and establishes a definite precedent in terms. However, where search is by warrant, there is no constitutional objection to the use of evidence obtained during it.[17]

The most important clause of the Fifth Amendment, the Due Process Clause, has been treated elsewhere, as it applies to the guarantees provided citizens of the United States. Here it will be necessary only to examine the cases where aliens are involved. As it happens, Justice Holmes' opinions on this precise point have been confined mainly to Chinese exclusion cases.

The guarantee of indictment by grand jury is involved in only one of his opinions,[18] where he speaks for a unanimous court in holding that proceedings were in proper form and preserved the constitutional rights of the prisoner when

---

[16] 201 U. S., 43.
[17] Schenck vs. U. S., Dec. March 3, 1919.
[18] Breese vs. Dickerson, 226 U. S., 1, 10.

the foreman handed an indictment to the judge in open court, though the jury was in another adjoining room.

Though latest in date, Tiaco vs. Forbes [19] sets forth Justice Holmes adherence to the doctrine that alien deportation proceedings are by their nature properly brought before executive officers. " It is admitted that sovereign states have inherent power to deport aliens, and seemingly that Congress is not deprived of this power by the Constitution of the United States. (Fong Tue Ting vs. U. S., 149 U. S., 698, 707, 728). . . . Furthermore, the very ground of the power in the necessities of public welfare shows that it may have to be exercised in a summary way through executive officers."

It has fallen to Justice Holmes to voice the opinion of the Supreme Court in two Chinese deportation cases which have gone far to settle the authority of administrative officials to decide finally on the merits of claims to admission by aliens, and to exclude by administrative processes those who claim United States citizenship, if such citizenship is not established to the satisfaction of departmental officers after an inquiry which does not plainly deny due process of law.

In U. S. vs. Sing Tuck,[20] a Chinaman who claimed United States citizenship, applied, during the course of proceedings before immigration officials, to a Federal Court for a writ of Habeas Corpus on the ground that the immigration officials had no final authority in his case. The specific question was not decided by the court, it being held that the administrative process must be carried through until the Secretary of the Treasury had definitely decided against the petitioner. At that time a petition for Habeas Corpus would be entertained by the Federal Court, which would decide whether the Secretary's decision was final as to those claiming citizenship, as it was to aliens.

By this case the way was opened for U. S. vs. Ju Toy.[21] The facts were similar to those in the Sing Tuck case, with an additional step of an appeal to the Secretary of Commerce, who had ruled against the appellant. There was a petition

---

[19] 228 U. S., 549.      [20] 194 U. S., 161.      [21] 198 U. S., 253.

for a writ of Habeas Corpus, and three questions were certified to the Supreme Court by the lower court. The two of them which are important were: (1) Should a Federal Court grant Habeas Corpus in the facts alleged, i. e., statement of citizenship, with offer of no new proof; (3) Should the decision of the Secretary of Commerce and Labor be regarded as final when citizen is at bar, or one claiming citizenship, it not being alleged in any of the three questions that anything irregular or unfair was done at any of the hearings granted.

The opinion of Justice Holmes holds that the first question is answered by U. S. vs. Sing Tuck: " A petition for habeas corpus ought not to be entertained unless the court is satisfied that the petitioner can make out at least a prima facie case." The Justice goes on to say: " This petition should have been denied on this ground, irrespective of what more we have to say, because it alleged nothing except citizenship. It disclosed neither abuse of authority nor the existence of evidence not laid before the Secretary."

As to the broad question of whether the decision of the Secretary is conclusive here, the opinion states that the Chinese Exclusion Act purports to make the Secretary the final judge " as well when it is citizenship as when it is domicil, and the belonging to a class excepted from the exclusion acts ". . . .

The statute has been upheld and enforced. . . . But the relevant portion being a single section, accomplishing all its results by the same general words must be valid as to all that it embraces, or altogether void. An exception of a class constitutionally exempted cannot be read into those general words merely for the purpose of saving what remains.

The petitioner, although physically within our boundaries, is to be regarded as if he had been stopped at the limit of our jurisdiction, and kept there while his right to enter was under debate. If, for the purpose of argument, we assume that the 5th Amendment applies to him, and that to deny entrance to a citizen is to deprive him of liberty, we nevertheless are of opinion that with regard to him due process of law does not require judicial trial.

In both of the above cases it is important to note that there is no allegation of improper hearing, or of any irregularities on the part of the immigration officials. In the final opinion which Justice Holmes pronounced in this class of cases, in Chin Yow vs. U. S.,[22] a Chinaman claiming citizenship had gone through all stages of the prescribed procedure, and was being held for deportation.  He petitioned for a writ of Habeas Corpus, alleging that he had been arbitrarily denied a proper hearing, that he was prevented from obtaining testimony on his own behalf, and that he could prove his citizenship on the merits.

Justice Holmes holds that if a writ is granted the issue must be confined to the allegation of the denial of a proper hearing.  If this be disproved, the merits certainly cannot be taken up.  The jurisdiction of the circuit court is established only by proving the fact of a hearing denying due process of law.  But, supposing that the allegation can be proved.  Can Habeas Corpus then give him the hearing on the merits which he has been denied?

As between the substantive right of citizens to enter and of persons alleging themselves to be citizens to have a chance to prove their allegation, on the one side, and the conclusiveness of the commissioner's fiat, on the other, when one or the other must give way, the latter must yield.  In such a case something must be done, and it naturally falls to be done by the courts.  In order to decide what, we must analyze a little.

If we regard the petitioner, as in Ju Toy's case it was said that he should be regarded, as if he had been stopped and kept at the limit of our jurisdiction (198 U. S., 263), still it would be difficult to say that he was not imprisoned, theoretically as well as practically when to turn him back meant that he must get into a vessel against his wish and be carried to China.  The case would not be that of a person simply prevented from going in one direction that he desired and has a right to take, all others being left open to him, a case in which the judges were not unanimous in Bird vs. Jones, 7, Q. B., 742.  But we need not speculate upon niceties.  It is true that the petitioner gains no additional right of entrance by being allowed to pass the frontier in custody for the determination of his case.  But, on the question whether he is wrongly imprisoned, we must look at the actual facts.  *De facto*, he is locked up until carried out of the country against his will.

The petitioner then is imprisoned for deportation without the process of law to which he is given a right.  Habeas Corpus is the usual remedy for unlawful imprisonment.  But, on the other hand, as yet the petitioner has not established his right to enter the country.  He is imprisoned only to prevent his entry, and an unconditional release would make the entry complete without the requisite proof.  The courts must deal with the matter somehow, and there seems to be no way so convenient as a trial of the merits

[22] 208 U. S., 8.

before the judge. If the petitioner proves his citizenship, a longer restraint would be illegal. If he fails, the order of deportation would remain in force.

Sustaining the contention that the upholding of a defendant's plea of limitations in a criminal case goes to the merits and is jeopardy, the decision delivered by Justice Holmes in U. S. vs. Oppenheimer [23] is interesting in part:

It cannot be that the safeguards of the person, so often and so rightfully mentioned with solemn reverence, are less than those that protect from a liability in debt.

The safeguard provided by the Constitution against the gravest abuses has tended to give the impression that when it did not apply in terms, there was no other principle that could. But the 5th Amendment was not intended to do away with what in the civil law is a fundamental principle of justice (Jeter vs. Hewitt, 22 How. 353, 364) in order, when a man once has been acquitted on the merits, to enable the government to prosecute him a second time.

In Kepner vs. United States,[24] Justice Holmes dissented from the court's decision on grounds that, at first glance, seem to be novel and difficult to explain. In this case, Kepner had been tried by an inferior court of the Philippine Islands for a criminal offense, and had been acquitted. The trial had not been before a jury. The government had appealed, and the Supreme Court of the Philippines had reversed the decision, finding Kepner guilty and imposing sentence.

The majority opinion held that the first trial had constituted jeopardy. "The weight of authority, as well as decisions of this court, have sanctioned the rule that a person has been in jeopardy when he is regularly charged with a crime before a tribunal properly organized and competent to try him; certainly so after acquittal."

Justice Holmes, who was joined in his opinion by Justices White and McKenna, upholds the view that the government constitutionally may be given the right of appeal in criminal cases, whereby errors of law in the lower court may be corrected, and a new trial ordered. He states that new trials are not to be differentiated from retrials, and that it is well established that, in proper cases, the latter are constitutional.

---

[23] 242 U. S., 85.
[24] 195 U. S., 100.

The jeopardy, from this point of view, is a continuing one, and does not cease with the erroneous verdict of the lower court, or become double when the appellate court orders a new trial. The constitutional prohibition against double jeopardy is to be interpreted as excluding a totally new case from trial where a man has once been tried on the same facts. It is intimated that an accused may be tried as many times in the same case as there are errors of law. There have been no fundamental cases on the point of self-incrimination on which Justice Holmes has expressed an opinion. One interesting statement of a phase of the question is to be found, however, in Johnson vs. United States.[25] The plaintiff in error had been a defendant in bankruptcy proceedings, during which his books were transferred under the law to a trustee. Evidence of his fraud was found in these books, he was charged with it in a criminal proceeding, and his books were offered in evidence against him. He was convicted, and appealed, claiming that the use of his books was equivalent to enforced self-incrimation contrary to the 5th Amendment. In his opinion, Justice Holmes says: " A party is privileged from producing the evidence, but not from its production. The transfer by bankruptcy is no different from a transfer by execution of a volume with a confession written on the fly leaf."

Further, the criminal cannot protect himself by getting legal title to his books. He must have both title and possession. While he himself retains the evidence he is protected, not otherwise: " If the documentary confession comes to a third hand *alio intuitu,* as this did, the use of it in court does not compel the defendant to be a witness against himself."

The depositing of a bankrupt's books with a receiver is not repugnant to the 5th Amendment because information may be got from them that will lead to investigations into the criminal acts of the bankrupt, and because the likely result of such investigations will be criminal prosecution.

[25] 228 U. S., 457.

" It is one of the misfortunes of bankruptcy if it follows crime." [26]

In a case where a coat was tried on a prisoner in court to prove that it fitted him, and therefore belonged to him, Justice Holmes said: [27] " But the prohibition of compelling a man in a criminal court to be a witness against himself is a prohibition of the use of physical or moral compulsion to extort communications from him, not an exclusion of his body as evidence when it may be material."

The fact that an official of a corporation had produced evidence from his books, under a subpoena and a legal guaranty that he would not be prosecuted as a result of such evidence, does not privilege him against prosecution as an officer of the corporation for other transactions concerning which he had given no testimony.[28]

Justice Holmes led four dissenting justices in attacks on the majority opinions in two recent cases in which the requirement of the 6th Amendment is raised, that the trial of a criminal case must be by a jury " of the State and district wherein the crime shall have been committed, which district shall have been previously ascertained by law."

In each case the prosecution was for conspiracy, the trials taking place where the overt acts in pursuance of the conspiracy were committed. The majority opinions held that the place of the overt act was the place of the conspiracy, and that the courts at the place where the acts were committed therefore had jurisdiction over the conspiracy. In Justice Holmes' view, and in the views of Justices Lurten, Hughes and Lamar, this is a plain misconception of the law, and there is no jurisdiction over the conspiracy given by the locus of the overt act. He says: [29] " But when they are

---

[26] Matter of Harris, 221 U. S., 274, 279. See Schenck vs. U. S., Dec. March 3, 1919, which cites Holt vs. U. S. as authority for holding that " the notion that evidence even directly proceeding from the defendant in a criminal proceeding is excluded in all cases by the 5th Amendment is plainly unsound."

[27] Holt vs. United States, 218 U. S., 245, 253, 254.

[28] Heike vs. United States, 227 U. S., 131.

[29] Brown vs. Elliott, 225 U. S., 392.

punished for being and not for doing, when the offense consists in no act beyond the osmose of mutual understanding, they should be punished only where they are,—only where the wrongful relation exists. . . . It does not follow from the defendant's liability in Omaha for certain results of their conspiracy that they can be tried there for the conspiracy itself."

In the other case,[30] the same idea is expressed: " The Constitution is not to be satisfied with a fiction. When a man causes an unlawful act, as in the case of a prohibited use of the mails, it needs no fiction to say that the crime is committed at the place of the act, wherever the man may be, Re Palliser, 136 U. S., 257. . . . But when the offense consists solely in a relation to other men with certain intent, it is pure fiction to say that the relation is maintained and present in the case supposed."

In a comparatively recent interpretation of the 8th Amendment,[31] forbidding " cruel and unusual punishments," the Supreme Court avowedly extended the previously understood meaning of that clause to a totally new significance, and established a precedent of a far-reaching importance. Justice White, Justice Holmes concurring with him, held a strong dissenting opinion, combatting the extension, and limiting the scope of the Amendment to its former meaning, that is: bodily torture or other punishments physically inhuman. The court's opinion included, under the prohibition, punishments that in the judgment of a court were not apportioned to the seriousness of the crime, or were " cruel and unusual " on account of length of sentence, attendant conditions, and severity. Such an interpretation is justified by analogy with the extension over mere words of the 14th Amendment and the Commerce Clause made by the Supreme Court in the past. Justice White's opposition to this reasoning is founded upon the facts in regard to the 8th Amendment which are revealed by history, namely, that it was meant only to apply

---

[30] Hyde vs. United States, 225 U. S., 347.
[31] Weems vs. United States, 217 U. S., 349, 382.

to punishments that were cruel and unusual physically, and that since the Declaration of Rights of 1688-1689, this meaning of the words has been accepted by legislatures and courts. He can find no warrant for such an unforeseen enlargement of the power of the courts. In concluding, he states that the greatest benefit from the Constitution comes from its general terms, which have allowed expansion; but that the court has always defended the idea that these general terms should not be made to include things that obviously are not meant to be covered, no matter how pressing otherwise.

This latter reasoning is consistent with Justice Holmes' declared principles of constitutional interpretation. He does not limit the Constitution to the words, or the exact picture its framers had in mind; but inquires what kind of evils they strove to prevent, not what specific evil. In other words, it is something of Marshall's method,—would the framers have changed the words of the clause if they had been confronted with the present case, so as to exclude it? The answer of Justices White and Holmes is that they would thus have changed the wording of the clause, since nothing in the history of the antecedents of the clause, or of the legislation enacted without its having been raised, gives ground for the belief that it aimed at the prohibition of anything except physical tortures.

It seems, indeed, that the decision of the court was a very wide departure from established precedent, which, though doubtless salutary in this case, gives to the courts a new veto power over legislative discretion in the matter of criminal law, a power construed out of the thin air of expediency into the 8th Amendment.

# INDEX

## VITA

Dorsey Richardson was born at Church Creek, Maryland, in 1896, and obtained his elementary education at private schools in Baltimore. He received the degree of Bachelor of Arts from The Johns Hopkins University in 1915. In the same year he entered the graduate department of The Johns Hopkins University, and pursued courses in Political Science, History and Law. He received the degree of Master of Arts in February, 1918, while absent in France. He served with the 17th Regiment, U. S. Field Artillery, Second Division, A. E. F., having been commissioned First Lieutenant, August 9, 1917. He served with the 2nd Division at the front, and was later with the Army of Occupation at Coblentz. He also served with the Baltic Relief Mission, and was assigned to the Peace Mission at Paris in August, 1919.